My Complete Diary

Season by Season
Five Aspects of Living

Chrystal V Benson, RN, MACN, MACMHN

BALBOA.
PRESS
A DIVISION OF HAY HOUSE

Balboa Press books may be ordered through booksellers or by contacting:

Balboa Press
A Division of Hay House
1663 Liberty Drive
Bloomington, IN 47403
www.balboapress.com.au
1 (877) 407-4847

Because of the dynamic nature of the Internet, any web addresses or links contained in this book may have changed since publication and may no longer be valid. The views expressed in this work are solely those of the author and do not necessarily reflect the views of the publisher, and the publisher hereby disclaims any responsibility for them.

The author of this book does not dispense medical advice or prescribe the use of any technique as a form of treatment for physical, emotional, or medical problems without the advice of a physician, either directly or indirectly. The intent of the author is only to offer information of a general nature to help you in your quest for emotional and spiritual well-being. In the event you use any of the information in this book for yourself, which is your constitutional right, the author and the publisher assume no responsibility for your actions.

Any people depicted in stock imagery provided by Getty Images are models, and such images are being used for illustrative purposes only. Certain stock imagery © Getty Images.

ISBN: 978-1-5043-1509-8 (sc)
ISBN: 978-1-5043-1513-5 (e)

Print information available on the last page.

Balboa Press rev. date: 10/22/2018

If you are in crisis, call your country's emergency phone number or attend your local hospital emergency department immediately.

Emergency numbers if you are in crisis and need immediate medical care

Australia	Emergency	000
Canada	Emergency	911
New Zealand	Emergency	111
United Kingdom	Emergency	999
United States of America	Emergency	911
International mobile phones	Emergency	112

Australian Mental Health Crisis Phone lines (State by State)

Australia	Australian Capital Territory	1800 629 354 and (02) 6205 1065
	New South Wales	1800 011 511
	Northern Territory	1800 682 288
	Queensland	1300 64 22 55
	South Australia	13 14 65
	Tasmania	1800 332 388
	Victoria	1300 60 60 24
	Western Australia	1300 555 788 metro 1800 676 822 Peel 1800 55 20 22 (Rural Link) (08) 9224 888

Canada Mental Health Crisis Phone line **1-888-353-2273.**

Web address for multiple crisis and support services state by state https://www.canada.ca/en/public-health/services/mental-health-services/mental-health-get-help.html

Canada	Alberta – Edmonton & Northern Alberta	1-800-232-7288
	Alberta - all	1-800-263-3045
	British Columbia	310-6789
	Manitoba Winnipeg	(204) 940-1781
	Interlake & Eastern	1-866-427-8628
	Prairie Mountain	1-866-332-3030
	Northern Region Thompson Hospital	(204) 677-2381
	Southern Health Sante Sud	1-888-310-4593
	New Brunswick	1-800-667-5005
	Newfoundland and Labrador	888-737 4668 (toll free)
	Northwest Territories	1-800-661-0844
	Nova Scotia	1-888-429-8167
	Nunvut	1-800-265-3333 (7pm-11pm)
	Ontario	1-888-353-2273
	Prince Edward Island	1-800-218-2885
	Quebec	1-866-APPELLE (277-3553)
	Saskatchewan - Saskatoon	(306) 933-6200
	Northern Saskatchewan	1-800-263-3045
	North East Saskatchewan	1-800-611-6349
	Hudson Bay and District	1-866-865-7274
	Prince Albert	(306) 764-1011
	Regina	(306) 525-5333

New Zealand Mental Health Crisis Phone line is **0800 611 116.**

United Kingdom Mental Health Crisis Phone line is **0800 068 4141.**

United States of America Mental Health America is **1-800-273-TALK (8255).**

Phone numbers are correct as of April 2018

Your notes

Contact persons & their phone numbers in case of emergency

Your Doctor

Your next of kin

Your case manager/counsellor/psychologist

Your specialist/clinic

Introduction

I work with clients who have chronic health, mental health, alcohol and other drugs issues. I created this three month diary to help track their own activities in daily life. I did this so that they could stay in charge of their quality of life. The World Health Organisation defines Quality of Life *"as an individual's perception of their position in life in the context of the culture and value systems in which they live and in relation to their goals, expectations, standards and concerns".*

Mackay and others described a new model of health care based on developing self-care, self-understanding and taking personal responsibility for your own health. Often, clients have treated me like I was the expert on their health. I am not the expert on their health, they are. This diary helped them to develop understanding on how their health conditions impacted their quality of life, and helped me to help them, and it can help you too. From their self knowledge came changes.

Please use this diary to track the 5 Aspects of Living that act as a barometer for how your life is going. You can show this to your counsellor, psychologist, therapist, case manager or Doctor as a way of revealing what your life is like at home, at work, with family and friends. Often when we get into our therapy session or our Doctor's appointment, we forget things that were important to communicate due to the normal anxiety we experience at that time. The diary acts as a prompt for your support person/s to ask questions and for you to share your activities since they last saw you. You can also use it to help advise them what you are planning to do until you see them again.

The 5 Aspects of Living are important measures to indicate how you are travelling in your life. They are:

- your diet – what did you eat and drink – how much and when;
- your sleep pattern and quality;
- exercise you have completed;
- your mood over the day; and
- your social contacts.

Each of these 5 Aspects reveal if things are on track in our self-caring behaviours. There are often anomalies that we don't understand. These anomalies are normal experiences as long as they do not continue to occur repetitively or persist for long periods of time. Everything that you put into your body - food, fluids, thoughts, emotions, and movements - has an impact. Take charge of these.

If we don't sleep well for many days at a time, something will give. If we are not eating well because we can't stomach something, we will lose weight and condition, and our immune system will suffer and eventually fail. If we overeat, we lose freedom of movement in our body.

We exercise to feel good, but there are many other ways of feeling good. We can listen to music, we can watch an inspiring movie, or we can meditate. It's best not to rely on just one thing to lift our mood. This diary is the first tool in your tool box. Gather as many as you can that work for you.

It's important to update the diary every day, whilst the events are still fresh in your mind. But don't panic if you miss a day – this says something too. It's important to review how the day went – so you can plan how to handle similar events in the future. Some days require solitude and some days we need busy activity. Consider what you liked and didn't like about the day.

Above all, be honest with yourself. This is not a test, it's a record for you to develop insight into what is impacting your life or illness. It helps free up our imagination to consider other ways to improve and enjoy life.

Some things to consider that impact our day come under the heading of HALTSSSS:

- Hungry (for food, love, attention)
- Angry (frustrated, upset)
- Lonely (boredom, sadness),
- Tired (emotionally, mentally, spiritually, physically, socially)
- Sick (in body, mind or feelings),
- Sad (anxious, low in mood)
- Sore (emotionally, mentally, spiritually, physically) and
- Sorry (embarrassed or ashamed).

It is normal that HALTSSSS influences how we react, but we risk losing control and our ability to function satisfactorily deteriorates. So, understanding what has influenced our day is vital to keeping ourselves well informed about our behaviour. Decide what you let impact you and talk about it.

Consider how you responded if you have had a lousy night's sleep, or missed lunch trying to pack too much in, or got annoyed at one of life's inconveniences. You are still responsible for your behaviour, however paying attention means you can adjust those areas that need improvement and repeat those things that help you function better and enjoy life. And don't forget to talk to others if you need to - friends, family, a health professional, counsellor, psychologist, therapist or Doctor.

When things are going badly, we increase our risk of lapse and relapse because there is an increase in our vulnerability and we start to make decisions based on **emotional reactivity**. This idea of normal fluctuations in our mental health is supported by Barker's Tidal Model, but **the Tidal model can apply to any health condition.** Keeping a separate journal to record your emotional responses is valuable; an exercise book will suffice. You can fully express your thoughts in that journal and you can keep it private if you wish.

This diary is intended to help you monitor **your 5 Aspects of Living** and repair or repeat your activities as needed. Palmer and others showed there is great value in keeping written plans to assist with recovery. I believe any chronic or episodic health issue or condition deserves attention to increase our self-understanding, thus we improve our lives and maintain our autonomy as much as possible.

At the back of the book are a Keeping Well Plan (**KWP**) and Relapse Prevention Plans (**RPP**). These need to be written by you to ensure that your voice, beliefs, opinions and attitudes are heard by yourself and others. You are responsible to develop these plans. So, it is personalised for you by you. you can change your **KWP** at any time as you develop greater self-understanding. When things are becoming tough, you can activate some of your ideas that you put in this plan to keep you on track.

There are 2 parts to the **Relapse Prevention Plan (RPP).**

Part One is for when things are starting to unravel and helps get you back on track.

Part Two is for when things have really gone downhill and you need more external support from health services, your case manager or a Crisis team. Part Two is designed to have your wishes for treatment expressed so that you feel you have some control over the circumstances and reduce the fear associated with being unwell and being unsure of what is happening. Part Two needs to be shared freely with any health service you contact if you are becoming unwell. Every 3 months you can revisit your plans and fine tune them to represent your unique needs and abilities and then share with those people most important in your journey.

I developed a three month diary to encourage reflection on our lives across the seasons as well as day to day. The ability to give a clear correlation between the months across many years can give great insight into anniversaries, weather influences, days of purpose or crisis and how they revisit us over time. I hope this diary becomes a vital and useful tool that you use over and over again to help you maximise your quality of life.

Further reading

Barker, P & Buchanan-Barker, P (2010), The Tidal Model of Mental health Recovery and Reclamation: Application in Acute Care Settings, Issues in Mental health Nursing, 31, 171-180.

Korsbek, L (2013), Illness insight and recovery: How important is Illness Insight in Peoples' Recovery Process? Psychiatric Rehabilitation Journal, 36(3) 222-225.

Mackay, s, Hatcher, D, Happell, B & Cleary, M (2013), Primary Health Care as a philosophical and practical framework for nursing education: Rhetoric or reality? Contemporary Nurse, 45(1), 79-84.

Palmer, V, Johnson, C, Furler, J, Densley, K, Portidiadis, M & Gunn, J (;2014), Written plans: an overlooked mechanism to develop recovery-oriented primary care in depression? Australian Journal of Primary Care, 20, 241-249.

World Health Organisation (2018) WHOQOL: Measuring Quality of Life, viewed 21 March 2018 http://www.who.int/healthinfo/survey/whoqol-qualityoflife/en/

Month of

| January | February | March |
| October | November | December |

April   May   June

July   August   September

Today is _____ Date: _____

Food diary for today: (include any alcohol intake)

Time	Meal	Food	How do you feel?
	Breakfast		
	Morning tea		
	Lunch		
	Afternoon tea		
	Dinner		
	Supper		
	Extra snacks		

Sleep diary:

How many hours?	Quality?	Notes

Rested/tired/restless/interruptions/dreams/thirsty/toilet/worrying/crying?

Exercise diary for today:

Time	Exercise type	How long for?	How do you feel?

Include incidental exercise like climbing stairs, cycling the kids to school or walking to shops.

Mood diary for today:

	6am	8am	10am	12pm	2pm	4pm	6pm	8pm	10 pm	12 am	2am	4am
+5												
+4												
+3												
+2												
+1												
0												
-1												
-2												
-3												
-4												
-5												

Chart your mood with a cross or star once or over the day.

Social contacts today:

Time	Who did you socialise with? Who are they to you?	How long for?	How do you feel?

Includes contacts at sports/gym, work, home and regular people you see during the day.

How did today go?

_____

_____

_____

What was the worst thing about today? _____

Did you talk with someone about this?   No   Yes

What was the **best thing** about today? _____

Did you talk with someone about this?   No   Yes

"Validate yourself by your beliefs and actions." Unknown

Today is _____ Date: _____

Food diary for today:

Time	Meal	Food	How do you feel?
	Breakfast		
	Morning tea		
	Lunch		
	Afternoon tea		
	Dinner		
	Supper		
	Extra snacks		

Sleep diary:

How many hours?	Quality?	Notes

Rested/tired/restless/interruptions/dreams/thirsty/toilet/worrying/crying?

Exercise diary for today:

Time	Exercise type	How long for?	How do you feel?

Include incidental exercise like climbing stairs, cycling the kids to school or walking to shops.

Mood diary for today:

	6am	8am	10am	12pm	2pm	4pm	6pm	8pm	10 pm	12 am	2am	4am
+5												
+4												
+3												
+2												
+1												
0												
-1												
-2												
-3												
-4												
-5												

Chart your mood with a cross or star either once or over the day.

Social contacts today:

Time	Who did you socialise with? Who are they to you?	How long for?	How do you feel?

Includes contacts at sports/gym, work, home and regular people you see during the day.

How did today go?

_____

_____

_____

What was the worst thing about today? _____

Did you talk with someone about this?   No   Yes

What was the **best thing** about today? _____

Did you talk with someone about this?   No   Yes

_____

"To be old and wise, we first have to be young and stupid." unknown

Today is _____ Date: _____

Food diary for today:

Time	Meal	Food	How do you feel?
	Breakfast		
	Morning tea		
	Lunch		
	Afternoon tea		
	Dinner		
	Supper		
	Extra snacks		

Sleep diary:

How many hours?	Quality?	Notes

Rested/tired/restless/interruptions/dreams/thirsty/toilet/worrying/crying?

Exercise diary for today:

Time	Exercise type	How long for?	How do you feel?

Include incidental exercise like climbing stairs, cycling the kids to school or walking to shops.

Mood diary for today:

	6am	8am	10am	12pm	2pm	4pm	6pm	8pm	10 pm	12 am	2am	4am
+5												
+4												
+3												
+2												
+1												
0												
-1												
-2												
-3												
-4												
-5												

Chart your mood with a cross or star either once or over the day.

Social contacts today:

Time	Who did you socialise with? Who are they to you?	How long for?	How do you feel?

Includes contacts at sports/gym, work, home and regular people you see during the day.

How did today go?

_____

_____

_____

What was the worst thing about today? _____

Did you talk with someone about this?   No   Yes

What was the **best thing** about today? _____

Did you talk with someone about this?   No   Yes

"We don't know who we are until we see what we can do." Martha Graham

Today is _____ Date: _____

Food diary for today:

Time	Meal	Food	How do you feel?
	Breakfast		
	Morning tea		
	Lunch		
	Afternoon tea		
	Dinner		
	Supper		
	Extra snacks		

Sleep diary:

How many hours?	Quality?	Notes

Rested/tired/restless/interruptions/dreams/thirsty/toilet/worrying/crying?

Exercise diary for today:

Time	Exercise type	How long for?	How do you feel?

Include incidental exercise like climbing stairs, cycling the kids to school or walking to shops.

Mood diary for today:

	6am	8am	10am	12pm	2pm	4pm	6pm	8pm	10 pm	12 am	2am	4am
+5												
+4												
+3												
+2												
+1												
0												
-1												
-2												
-3												
-4												
-5												

Chart your mood with a cross or star either once or over the day.

Social contacts today:

Time	Who did you socialise with? Who are they to you?	How long for?	How do you feel?

Includes contacts at sports/gym, work, home and regular people you see during the day.

How did today go?

_____

_____

_____

What was the worst thing about today? _____

Did you talk with someone about this?   No   Yes

What was the **best thing** about today? _____

Did you talk with someone about this?   No   Yes

"If you are not prepared to be wrong, you will never come up with anything original." Ken Robertson

Today is _____ Date: _____

Food diary for today:

Time	Meal	Food	How do you feel?
	Breakfast		
	Morning tea		
	Lunch		
	Afternoon tea		
	Dinner		
	Supper		
	Extra snacks		

Sleep diary:

How many hours?	Quality?	Notes

Rested/tired/restless/interruptions/dreams/thirsty/toilet/worrying/crying?

Exercise diary for today:

Time	Exercise type	How long for?	How do you feel?

Include incidental exercise like climbing stairs, cycling the kids to school or walking to shops.

Mood diary for today:

	6am	8am	10am	12pm	2pm	4pm	6pm	8pm	10 pm	12 am	2am	4am
+5												
+4												
+3												
+2												
+1												
0												
-1												
-2												
-3												
-4												
-5												

Chart your mood with a cross or star either once or over the day.

Social contacts today:

Time	Who did you socialise with? Who are they to you?	How long for?	How do you feel?

Includes contacts at sports/gym, work, home and regular people you see during the day.

How did today go?

_____

_____

_____

What was the worst thing about today? _____

Did you talk with someone about this?   No   Yes

What was the **best thing** about today? _____

Did you talk with someone about this?   No   Yes

"Don't let yesterday take up too much of today." Will Roger

Today is _____ Date: _____

Food diary for today:

Time	Meal	Food	How do you feel?
	Breakfast		
	Morning tea		
	Lunch		
	Afternoon tea		
	Dinner		
	Supper		
	Extra snacks		

Sleep diary:

How many hours?	Quality?	Notes

Rested/tired/restless/interruptions/dreams/thirsty/toilet/worrying/crying?

Exercise diary for today:

Time	Exercise type	How long for?	How do you feel?

Include incidental exercise like climbing stairs, cycling the kids to school or walking to shops.

Mood diary for today:

	6am	8am	10am	12pm	2pm	4pm	6pm	8pm	10 pm	12 am	2am	4am
+5												
+4												
+3												
+2												
+1												
0												
-1												
-2												
-3												
-4												
-5												

Chart your mood with a cross or star either once or over the day.

Social contacts today:

Time	Who did you socialise with? Who are they to you?	How long for?	How do you feel?

Includes contacts at sports/gym, work, home and regular people you see during the day.

How did today go?

_____

_____

_____

What was the worst thing about today? _____

Did you talk with someone about this?   No   Yes

What was the **best thing** about today? _____

Did you talk with someone about this?   No   Yes

_____

"Sometimes, that's good enough for now." Chrystal V Benson

Today is _____ Date: _____

Food diary for today:

Time	Meal	Food	How do you feel?
	Breakfast		
	Morning tea		
	Lunch		
	Afternoon tea		
	Dinner		
	Supper		
	Extra snacks		

Sleep diary:

How many hours?	Quality?	Notes

Rested/tired/restless/interruptions/dreams/thirsty/toilet/worrying/crying?

Exercise diary for today:

Time	Exercise type	How long for?	How do you feel?

Include incidental exercise like climbing stairs, cycling the kids to school or walking to shops.

Mood diary for today:

	6am	8am	10am	12pm	2pm	4pm	6pm	8pm	10 pm	12 am	2am	4am
+5												
+4												
+3												
+2												
+1												
0												
-1												
-2												
-3												
-4												
-5												

Chart your mood with a cross or star either once or over the day.

Social contacts today:

Time	Who did you socialise with? Who are they to you?	How long for?	How do you feel?

Includes contacts at sports/gym, work, home and regular people you see during the day.

How did today go?

_____

_____

_____

What was the worst thing about today? _____

Did you talk with someone about this?   No   Yes

What was the **best thing** about today? _____

Did you talk with someone about this?   No   Yes

_____

"Kindness is like snow. It beautifies everything it covers." Kahlil Gibran

Today is _____ Date: _____

Food diary for today:

Time	Meal	Food	How do you feel?
	Breakfast		
	Morning tea		
	Lunch		
	Afternoon tea		
	Dinner		
	Supper		
	Extra snacks		

Sleep diary:

How many hours?	Quality?	Notes

Rested/tired/restless/interruptions/dreams/thirsty/toilet/worrying/crying?

Exercise diary for today:

Time	Exercise type	How long for?	How do you feel?

Include incidental exercise like climbing stairs, cycling the kids to school or walking to shops.

Mood diary for today:

	6am	8am	10am	12pm	2pm	4pm	6pm	8pm	10 pm	12 am	2am	4am
+5												
+4												
+3												
+2												
+1												
0												
-1												
-2												
-3												
-4												
-5												

Chart your mood with a cross or star either once or over the day.

Social contacts today:

Time	Who did you socialise with? Who are they to you?	How long for?	How do you feel?

Includes contacts at sports/gym, work, home and regular people you see during the day.

How did today go?

_____

_____

_____

What was the worst thing about today? _____

Did you talk with someone about this?   No   Yes

What was the **best thing** about today? _____

Did you talk with someone about this?   No   Yes

_____

"Challenge your assumptions, or they will challenge you.' Lissa Boles

Today is _____ Date: _____

Food diary for today:

Time	Meal	Food	How do you feel?
	Breakfast		
	Morning tea		
	Lunch		
	Afternoon tea		
	Dinner		
	Supper		
	Extra snacks		

Sleep diary:

How many hours?	Quality?	Notes

Rested/tired/restless/interruptions/dreams/thirsty/toilet/worrying/crying?

Exercise diary for today:

Time	Exercise type	How long for?	How do you feel?

Include incidental exercise like climbing stairs, cycling the kids to school or walking to shops.

Mood diary for today:

	6am	8am	10am	12pm	2pm	4pm	6pm	8pm	10 pm	12 am	2am	4am
+5												
+4												
+3												
+2												
+1												
0												
-1												
-2												
-3												
-4												
-5												

Chart your mood with a cross or star either once or over the day.

Social contacts today:

Time	Who did you socialise with? Who are they to you?	How long for?	How do you feel?

Includes contacts at sports/gym, work, home and regular people you see during the day.

How did today go?

_____

_____

_____

What was the worst thing about today? _____

Did you talk with someone about this?   No   Yes

What was the **best thing** about today? _____

Did you talk with someone about this?   No   Yes

"It's impossible to feel grateful and depressed at the same time."
Naomi Williams

Today is _____ Date: _____

Food diary for today:

Time	Meal	Food	How do you feel?
	Breakfast		
	Morning tea		
	Lunch		
	Afternoon tea		
	Dinner		
	Supper		
	Extra snacks		

Sleep diary:

How many hours?	Quality?	Notes

Rested/tired/restless/interruptions/dreams/thirsty/toilet/worrying/crying?

Exercise diary for today:

Time	Exercise type	How long for?	How do you feel?

Include incidental exercise like climbing stairs, cycling the kids to school or walking to shops.

Mood diary for today:

	6am	8am	10am	12pm	2pm	4pm	6pm	8pm	10 pm	12 am	2am	4am
+5												
+4												
+3												
+2												
+1												
0												
-1												
-2												
-3												
-4												
-5												

Chart your mood with a cross or star either once or over the day.

Social contacts today:

Time	Who did you socialise with? Who are they to you?	How long for?	How do you feel?

Includes contacts at sports/gym, work, home and regular people you see during the day.

How did today go?

_____

_____

_____

What was the worst thing about today? _____

Did you talk with someone about this?   No   Yes

What was the **best thing** about today? _____

Did you talk with someone about this?   No   Yes

_____

"Laughter is an instant vacation." Milton Berle

Today is _____ Date: _____

Food diary for today:

Time	Meal	Food	How do you feel?
	Breakfast		
	Morning tea		
	Lunch		
	Afternoon tea		
	Dinner		
	Supper		
	Extra snacks		

Sleep diary:

How many hours?	Quality?	Notes

Rested/tired/restless/interruptions/dreams/thirsty/toilet/worrying/crying?

Exercise diary for today:

Time	Exercise type	How long for?	How do you feel?

Include incidental exercise like climbing stairs, cycling the kids to school or walking to shops.

Mood diary for today:

	6am	8am	10am	12pm	2pm	4pm	6pm	8pm	10 pm	12 am	2am	4am
+5												
+4												
+3												
+2												
+1												
0												
-1												
-2												
-3												
-4												
-5												

Chart your mood with a cross or star either once or over the day.

Social contacts today:

Time	Who did you socialise with? Who are they to you?	How long for?	How do you feel?

Includes contacts at sports/gym, work, home and regular people you see during the day.

How did today go?

_____

_____

_____

What was the worst thing about today? _____

Did you talk with someone about this?   No   Yes

What was the **best thing** about today? _____

Did you talk with someone about this?   No   Yes

_____

"Today's mighty oak is yesterday's nut that held its ground." David Icke

Today is _____ Date: _____

Food diary for today:

Time	Meal	Food	How do you feel?
	Breakfast		
	Morning tea		
	Lunch		
	Afternoon tea		
	Dinner		
	Supper		
	Extra snacks		

Sleep diary:

How many hours?	Quality?	Notes

Rested/tired/restless/interruptions/dreams/thirsty/toilet/worrying/crying?

Exercise diary for today:

Time	Exercise type	How long for?	How do you feel?

Include incidental exercise like climbing stairs, cycling the kids to school or walking to shops.

Mood diary for today:

	6am	8am	10am	12pm	2pm	4pm	6pm	8pm	10 pm	12 am	2am	4am
+5												
+4												
+3												
+2												
+1												
0												
-1												
-2												
-3												
-4												
-5												

Chart your mood with a cross or star either once or over the day.

Social contacts today:

Time	Who did you socialise with? Who are they to you?	How long for?	How do you feel?

Includes contacts at sports/gym, work, home and regular people you see during the day.

How did today go?

_____

_____

_____

What was the worst thing about today? _____

Did you talk with someone about this?   No   Yes

What was the **best thing** about today? _____

Did you talk with someone about this?   No   Yes

"Nothing in excess." Gates of Delphi

Today is _____ Date: _____

Food diary for today:

Time	Meal	Food	How do you feel?
	Breakfast		
	Morning tea		
	Lunch		
	Afternoon tea		
	Dinner		
	Supper		
	Extra snacks		

Sleep diary:

How many hours?	Quality?	Notes

Rested/tired/restless/interruptions/dreams/thirsty/toilet/worrying/crying?

Exercise diary for today:

Time	Exercise type	How long for?	How do you feel?

Include incidental exercise like climbing stairs, cycling the kids to school or walking to shops.

Mood diary for today:

	6am	8am	10am	12pm	2pm	4pm	6pm	8pm	10 pm	12 am	2am	4am
+5												
+4												
+3												
+2												
+1												
0												
-1												
-2												
-3												
-4												
-5												

Chart your mood with a cross or star either once or over the day.

Social contacts today:

Time	Who did you socialise with? Who are they to you?	How long for?	How do you feel?

Includes contacts at sports/gym, work, home and regular people you see during the day.

How did today go?

_____

_____

_____

What was the worst thing about today? _____

Did you talk with someone about this?   No   Yes

What was the **best thing** about today? _____

Did you talk with someone about this?   No   Yes

"Don't believe everything you think." Unknown

Today is _____ Date: _____

Food diary for today:

Time	Meal	Food	How do you feel?
	Breakfast		
	Morning tea		
	Lunch		
	Afternoon tea		
	Dinner		
	Supper		
	Extra snacks		

Sleep diary:

How many hours?	Quality?	Notes

Rested/tired/restless/interruptions/dreams/thirsty/toilet/worrying/crying?

Exercise diary for today:

Time	Exercise type	How long for?	How do you feel?

Include incidental exercise like climbing stairs, cycling the kids to school or walking to shops.

Mood diary for today:

	6am	8am	10am	12pm	2pm	4pm	6pm	8pm	10 pm	12 am	2am	4am
+5												
+4												
+3												
+2												
+1												
0												
-1												
-2												
-3												
-4												
-5												

Chart your mood with a cross or star either once or over the day.

Social contacts today:

Time	Who did you socialise with? Who are they to you?	How long for?	How do you feel?

Includes contacts at sports/gym, work, home and regular people you see during the day.

How did today go?

_____

_____

_____

What was the worst thing about today? _____

Did you talk with someone about this?   No   Yes

What was the **best thing** about today? _____

Did you talk with someone about this?   No   Yes

"Courage is grace under pressure." Ernest Hemingway

Today is _____ Date: _____

Food diary for today:

Time	Meal	Food	How do you feel?
	Breakfast		
	Morning tea		
	Lunch		
	Afternoon tea		
	Dinner		
	Supper		
	Extra snacks		

Sleep diary:

How many hours?	Quality?	Notes

Rested/tired/restless/interruptions/dreams/thirsty/toilet/worrying/crying?

Exercise diary for today:

Time	Exercise type	How long for?	How do you feel?

Include incidental exercise like climbing stairs, cycling the kids to school or walking to shops.

Mood diary for today:

	6am	8am	10am	12pm	2pm	4pm	6pm	8pm	10 pm	12 am	2am	4am
+5												
+4												
+3												
+2												
+1												
0												
-1												
-2												
-3												
-4												
-5												

Chart your mood with a cross or star either once or over the day.

Social contacts today:

Time	Who did you socialise with? Who are they to you?	How long for?	How do you feel?

Includes contacts at sports/gym, work, home and regular people you see during the day.

How did today go?

_____

_____

_____

What was the worst thing about today? _____

Did you talk with someone about this?   No   Yes

What was the **best thing** about today? _____

Did you talk with someone about this?   No   Yes

_____

"Beautiful minds inspire others." Unknown

Today is _____ Date: _____

Food diary for today:

Time	Meal	Food	How do you feel?
	Breakfast		
	Morning tea		
	Lunch		
	Afternoon tea		
	Dinner		
	Supper		
	Extra snacks		

Sleep diary:

How many hours?	Quality?	Notes

Rested/tired/restless/interruptions/dreams/thirsty/toilet/worrying/crying?

Exercise diary for today:

Time	Exercise type	How long for?	How do you feel?

Include incidental exercise like climbing stairs, cycling the kids to school or walking to shops.

Mood diary for today:

	6am	8am	10am	12pm	2pm	4pm	6pm	8pm	10 pm	12 am	2am	4am
+5												
+4												
+3												
+2												
+1												
0												
-1												
-2												
-3												
-4												
-5												

Chart your mood with a cross or star either once or over the day.

Social contacts today:

Time	Who did you socialise with? Who are they to you?	How long for?	How do you feel?

Includes contacts at sports/gym, work, home and regular people you see during the day.

How did today go?

_____

_____

_____

What was the worst thing about today? _____

Did you talk with someone about this?   No   Yes

What was the **best thing** about today? _____

Did you talk with someone about this?   No   Yes

"What other's think of you is none of your business." Unknown

Today is _____ Date: _____

Food diary for today:

Time	Meal	Food	How do you feel?
	Breakfast		
	Morning tea		
	Lunch		
	Afternoon tea		
	Dinner		
	Supper		
	Extra snacks		

Sleep diary:

How many hours?	Quality?	Notes

Rested/tired/restless/interruptions/dreams/thirsty/toilet/worrying/crying?

Exercise diary for today:

Time	Exercise type	How long for?	How do you feel?

Include incidental exercise like climbing stairs, cycling the kids to school or walking to shops.

Mood diary for today:

	6am	8am	10am	12pm	2pm	4pm	6pm	8pm	10 pm	12 am	2am	4am
+5												
+4												
+3												
+2												
+1												
0												
-1												
-2												
-3												
-4												
-5												

Chart your mood with a cross or star either once or over the day.

Social contacts today:

Time	Who did you socialise with? Who are they to you?	How long for?	How do you feel?

Includes contacts at sports/gym, work, home and regular people you see during the day.

How did today go?

_____

_____

_____

What was the worst thing about today? _____

Did you talk with someone about this?   No   Yes

What was the **best thing** about today? _____

Did you talk with someone about this?   No   Yes

"Genuine compassion must have both wisdom and loving kindness."
The Dalai Lama

Today is _____ Date: _____

Food diary for today:

Time	Meal	Food	How do you feel?
	Breakfast		
	Morning tea		
	Lunch		
	Afternoon tea		
	Dinner		
	Supper		
	Extra snacks		

Sleep diary:

How many hours?	Quality?	Notes

Rested/tired/restless/interruptions/dreams/thirsty/toilet/worrying/crying?

Exercise diary for today:

Time	Exercise type	How long for?	How do you feel?

Include incidental exercise like climbing stairs, cycling the kids to school or walking to shops.

Mood diary for today:

	6am	8am	10am	12pm	2pm	4pm	6pm	8pm	10 pm	12 am	2am	4am
+5												
+4												
+3												
+2												
+1												
0												
-1												
-2												
-3												
-4												
-5												

Chart your mood with a cross or star either once or over the day.

Social contacts today:

Time	Who did you socialise with? Who are they to you?	How long for?	How do you feel?

Includes contacts at sports/gym, work, home and regular people you see during the day.

How did today go?

_____

_____

_____

What was the worst thing about today? _____

Did you talk with someone about this?   No   Yes

What was the **best thing** about today? _____

Did you talk with someone about this?   No   Yes

_____

"If you get your knickers in a twist, it's still your knickers."
Chrystal V Benson

Today is _____ Date: _____

Food diary for today:

Time	Meal	Food	How do you feel?
	Breakfast		
	Morning tea		
	Lunch		
	Afternoon tea		
	Dinner		
	Supper		
	Extra snacks		

Sleep diary:

How many hours?	Quality?	Notes

Rested/tired/restless/interruptions/dreams/thirsty/toilet/worrying/crying?

Exercise diary for today:

Time	Exercise type	How long for?	How do you feel?

Include incidental exercise like climbing stairs, cycling the kids to school or walking to shops.

Mood diary for today:

	6am	8am	10am	12pm	2pm	4pm	6pm	8pm	10 pm	12 am	2am	4am
+5												
+4												
+3												
+2												
+1												
0												
-1												
-2												
-3												
-4												
-5												

Chart your mood with a cross or star either once or over the day.

Social contacts today:

Time	Who did you socialise with? Who are they to you?	How long for?	How do you feel?

Includes contacts at sports/gym, work, home and regular people you see during the day.

How did today go?

_____

_____

_____

What was the worst thing about today? _____

Did you talk with someone about this?   No   Yes

What was the **best thing** about today? _____

Did you talk with someone about this?   No   Yes

_____

*"Gaze upward, look inward, reach outward,
press forward." Thomas S. Monson*

Today is _____ Date: _____

Food diary for today:

Time	Meal	Food	How do you feel?
	Breakfast		
	Morning tea		
	Lunch		
	Afternoon tea		
	Dinner		
	Supper		
	Extra snacks		

Sleep diary:

How many hours?	Quality?	Notes

Rested/tired/restless/interruptions/dreams/thirsty/toilet/worrying/crying?

Exercise diary for today:

Time	Exercise type	How long for?	How do you feel?

Include incidental exercise like climbing stairs, cycling the kids to school or walking to shops.

Mood diary for today:

	6am	8am	10am	12pm	2pm	4pm	6pm	8pm	10 pm	12 am	2am	4am
+5												
+4												
+3												
+2												
+1												
0												
-1												
-2												
-3												
-4												
-5												

Chart your mood with a cross or star either once or over the day.

Social contacts today:

Time	Who did you socialise with? Who are they to you?	How long for?	How do you feel?

Includes contacts at sports/gym, work, home and regular people you see during the day.

How did today go?

_____

_____

_____

What was the worst thing about today? _____

Did you talk with someone about this?   No   Yes

What was the **best thing** about today? _____

Did you talk with someone about this?   No   Yes

"Mistakes are proof that you are trying." Unknown

Today is _____ Date: _____

Food diary for today:

Time	Meal	Food	How do you feel?
	Breakfast		
	Morning tea		
	Lunch		
	Afternoon tea		
	Dinner		
	Supper		
	Extra snacks		

Sleep diary:

How many hours?	Quality?	Notes

Rested/tired/restless/interruptions/dreams/thirsty/toilet/worrying/crying?

Exercise diary for today:

Time	Exercise type	How long for?	How do you feel?

Include incidental exercise like climbing stairs, cycling the kids to school or walking to shops.

Mood diary for today:

	6am	8am	10am	12pm	2pm	4pm	6pm	8pm	10 pm	12 am	2am	4am
+5												
+4												
+3												
+2												
+1												
0												
-1												
-2												
-3												
-4												
-5												

Chart your mood with a cross or star either once or over the day.

Social contacts today:

Time	Who did you socialise with? Who are they to you?	How long for?	How do you feel?

Includes contacts at sports/gym, work, home and regular people you see during the day.

How did today go?

_____

_____

_____

What was the worst thing about today? _____

Did you talk with someone about this?   No   Yes

What was the **best thing** about today? _____

Did you talk with someone about this?   No   Yes

"When you are about to give up, think how you feel in three months' time. Still giving up?" Unknown

Today is _____ Date: _____

Food diary for today:

Time	Meal	Food	How do you feel?
	Breakfast		
	Morning tea		
	Lunch		
	Afternoon tea		
	Dinner		
	Supper		
	Extra snacks		

Sleep diary:

How many hours?	Quality?	Notes

Rested/tired/restless/interruptions/dreams/thirsty/toilet/worrying/crying?

Exercise diary for today:

Time	Exercise type	How long for?	How do you feel?

Include incidental exercise like climbing stairs, cycling the kids to school or walking to shops.

Mood diary for today:

	6am	8am	10am	12pm	2pm	4pm	6pm	8pm	10 pm	12 am	2am	4am
+5												
+4												
+3												
+2												
+1												
0												
-1												
-2												
-3												
-4												
-5												

Chart your mood with a cross or star either once or over the day.

Social contacts today:

Time	Who did you socialise with? Who are they to you?	How long for?	How do you feel?

Includes contacts at sports/gym, work, home and regular people you see during the day.

How did today go?

_____

_____

_____

What was the worst thing about today? _____

Did you talk with someone about this?   No   Yes

What was the **best thing** about today? _____

Did you talk with someone about this?   No   Yes

_____

"We are all broken, that's how the light gets in." Ernest Hemingway

Today is _____ Date: _____

Food diary for today:

Time	Meal	Food	How do you feel?
	Breakfast		
	Morning tea		
	Lunch		
	Afternoon tea		
	Dinner		
	Supper		
	Extra snacks		

Sleep diary:

How many hours?	Quality?	Notes

Rested/tired/restless/interruptions/dreams/thirsty/toilet/worrying/crying?

Exercise diary for today:

Time	Exercise type	How long for?	How do you feel?

Include incidental exercise like climbing stairs, cycling the kids to school or walking to shops.

Mood diary for today:

	6am	8am	10am	12pm	2pm	4pm	6pm	8pm	10 pm	12 am	2am	4am
+5												
+4												
+3												
+2												
+1												
0												
-1												
-2												
-3												
-4												
-5												

Chart your mood with a cross or star either once or over the day.

Social contacts today:

Time	Who did you socialise with? Who are they to you?	How long for?	How do you feel?

Includes contacts at sports/gym, work, home and regular people you see during the day.

How did today go?

_____

_____

_____

What was the worst thing about today? _____

Did you talk with someone about this?   No   Yes

What was the **best thing** about today? _____

Did you talk with someone about this?   No   Yes

"Patience is not about waiting, but having the right attitude when you are waiting." Unknown

Today is _____ Date: _____

Food diary for today:

Time	Meal	Food	How do you feel?
	Breakfast		
	Morning tea		
	Lunch		
	Afternoon tea		
	Dinner		
	Supper		
	Extra snacks		

Sleep diary:

How many hours?	Quality?	Notes

Rested/tired/restless/interruptions/dreams/thirsty/toilet/worrying/crying?

Exercise diary for today:

Time	Exercise type	How long for?	How do you feel?

Include incidental exercise like climbing stairs, cycling the kids to school or walking to shops.

Mood diary for today:

	6am	8am	10am	12pm	2pm	4pm	6pm	8pm	10 pm	12 am	2am	4am
+5												
+4												
+3												
+2												
+1												
0												
-1												
-2												
-3												
-4												
-5												

Chart your mood with a cross or star either once or over the day.

Social contacts today:

Time	Who did you socialise with? Who are they to you?	How long for?	How do you feel?

Includes contacts at sports/gym, work, home and regular people you see during the day.

How did today go?

_____

_____

_____

What was the worst thing about today? _____

Did you talk with someone about this?   No   Yes

What was the **best thing** about today? _____

Did you talk with someone about this?   No   Yes

"The best teachers are those that tell you where to look, but not what to see." Unknown

Today is _____ Date: _____

Food diary for today:

Time	Meal	Food	How do you feel?
	Breakfast		
	Morning tea		
	Lunch		
	Afternoon tea		
	Dinner		
	Supper		
	Extra snacks		

Sleep diary:

How many hours?	Quality?	Notes

Rested/tired/restless/interruptions/dreams/thirsty/toilet/worrying/crying?

Exercise diary for today:

Time	Exercise type	How long for?	How do you feel?

Include incidental exercise like climbing stairs, cycling the kids to school or walking to shops.

Mood diary for today:

	6am	8am	10am	12pm	2pm	4pm	6pm	8pm	10 pm	12 am	2am	4am
+5												
+4												
+3												
+2												
+1												
0												
-1												
-2												
-3												
-4												
-5												

Chart your mood with a cross or star either once or over the day.

Social contacts today:

Time	Who did you socialise with? Who are they to you?	How long for?	How do you feel?

Includes contacts at sports/gym, work, home and regular people you see during the day.

How did today go?

_____

_____

_____

What was the worst thing about today? _____

Did you talk with someone about this?   No   Yes

What was the **best thing** about today? _____

Did you talk with someone about this?   No   Yes

_____

"Where your attention is, is where your attention goes." Chrystal V Benson

Today is _____ Date: _____

Food diary for today:

Time	Meal	Food	How do you feel?
	Breakfast		
	Morning tea		
	Lunch		
	Afternoon tea		
	Dinner		
	Supper		
	Extra snacks		

Sleep diary:

How many hours?	Quality?	Notes

Rested/tired/restless/interruptions/dreams/thirsty/toilet/worrying/crying?

Exercise diary for today:

Time	Exercise type	How long for?	How do you feel?

Include incidental exercise like climbing stairs, cycling the kids to school or walking to shops.

Mood diary for today:

	6am	8am	10am	12pm	2pm	4pm	6pm	8pm	10 pm	12 am	2am	4am
+5												
+4												
+3												
+2												
+1												
0												
-1												
-2												
-3												
-4												
-5												

Chart your mood with a cross or star either once or over the day.

Social contacts today:

Time	Who did you socialise with? Who are they to you?	How long for?	How do you feel?

Includes contacts at sports/gym, work, home and regular people you see during the day.

How did today go?

_____

_____

_____

What was the worst thing about today? _____

Did you talk with someone about this?   No   Yes

What was the **best thing** about today? _____

Did you talk with someone about this?   No   Yes

"Children are great imitators, give them something
or someone great to imitate." Unknown

Today is _____ Date: _____

Food diary for today:

Time	Meal	Food	How do you feel?
	Breakfast		
	Morning tea		
	Lunch		
	Afternoon tea		
	Dinner		
	Supper		
	Extra snacks		

Sleep diary:

How many hours?	Quality?	Notes

Rested/tired/restless/interruptions/dreams/thirsty/toilet/worrying/crying?

Exercise diary for today:

Time	Exercise type	How long for?	How do you feel?

Include incidental exercise like climbing stairs, cycling the kids to school or walking to shops.

Mood diary for today:

	6am	8am	10am	12pm	2pm	4pm	6pm	8pm	10 pm	12 am	2am	4am
+5												
+4												
+3												
+2												
+1												
0												
-1												
-2												
-3												
-4												
-5												

Chart your mood with a cross or star either once or over the day.

Social contacts today:

Time	Who did you socialise with? Who are they to you?	How long for?	How do you feel?

Includes contacts at sports/gym, work, home and regular people you see during the day.

How did today go?

_____

_____

_____

What was the worst thing about today? _____

Did you talk with someone about this?   No   Yes

What was the **best thing** about today? _____

Did you talk with someone about this?   No   Yes

"I never dreamed of success, I worked for it." Estee Lauder

Today is _____ Date: _____

Food diary for today:

Time	Meal	Food	How do you feel?
	Breakfast		
	Morning tea		
	Lunch		
	Afternoon tea		
	Dinner		
	Supper		
	Extra snacks		

Sleep diary:

How many hours?	Quality?	Notes

Rested/tired/restless/interruptions/dreams/thirsty/toilet/worrying/crying?

Exercise diary for today:

Time	Exercise type	How long for?	How do you feel?

Include incidental exercise like climbing stairs, cycling the kids to school or walking to shops.

Mood diary for today:

	6am	8am	10am	12pm	2pm	4pm	6pm	8pm	10 pm	12 am	2am	4am
+5												
+4												
+3												
+2												
+1												
0												
-1												
-2												
-3												
-4												
-5												

Chart your mood with a cross or star either once or over the day.

Social contacts today:

Time	Who did you socialise with? Who are they to you?	How long for?	How do you feel?

Includes contacts at sports/gym, work, home and regular people you see during the day.

How did today go?

_____

_____

_____

What was the worst thing about today? _____

Did you talk with someone about this?   No   Yes

What was the **best thing** about today? _____

Did you talk with someone about this?   No   Yes

_____

"When it rains look for rainbows, when it is dark, look for
stars – look for beauty all around you." Unknown

Today is _____ Date: _____

Food diary for today:

Time	Meal	Food	How do you feel?
	Breakfast		
	Morning tea		
	Lunch		
	Afternoon tea		
	Dinner		
	Supper		
	Extra snacks		

Sleep diary:

How many hours?	Quality?	Notes

Rested/tired/restless/interruptions/dreams/thirsty/toilet/worrying/crying?

Exercise diary for today:

Time	Exercise type	How long for?	How do you feel?

Include incidental exercise like climbing stairs, cycling the kids to school or walking to shops.

Mood diary for today:

	6am	8am	10am	12pm	2pm	4pm	6pm	8pm	10 pm	12 am	2am	4am
+5												
+4												
+3												
+2												
+1												
0												
-1												
-2												
-3												
-4												
-5												

Chart your mood with a cross or star either once or over the day.

Social contacts today:

Time	Who did you socialise with? Who are they to you?	How long for?	How do you feel?

Includes contacts at sports/gym, work, home and regular people you see during the day.

How did today go?

_____

_____

_____

What was the worst thing about today? _____

Did you talk with someone about this?   No   Yes

What was the **best thing** about today? _____

Did you talk with someone about this?   No   Yes

"Do the best you can until you know better, then when you know better, do better." Maya Angelou

Today is _____ Date: _____

Food diary for today:

Time	Meal	Food	How do you feel?
	Breakfast		
	Morning tea		
	Lunch		
	Afternoon tea		
	Dinner		
	Supper		
	Extra snacks		

Sleep diary:

How many hours?	Quality?	Notes

Rested/tired/restless/interruptions/dreams/thirsty/toilet/worrying/crying?

Exercise diary for today:

Time	Exercise type	How long for?	How do you feel?

Include incidental exercise like climbing stairs, cycling the kids to school or walking to shops.

Mood diary for today:

	6am	8am	10am	12pm	2pm	4pm	6pm	8pm	10 pm	12 am	2am	4am
+5												
+4												
+3												
+2												
+1												
0												
-1												
-2												
-3												
-4												
-5												

Chart your mood with a cross or star either once or over the day.

Social contacts today:

Time	Who did you socialise with? Who are they to you?	How long for?	How do you feel?

Includes contacts at sports/gym, work, home and regular people you see during the day.

How did today go?

_____

_____

_____

What was the worst thing about today? _____

Did you talk with someone about this?   No   Yes

What was the **best thing** about today? _____

Did you talk with someone about this?   No   Yes

_____

"The pessimist sees difficulty in every opportunity, the optimist sees opportunity in every difficulty." Winston Churchill

Today is _____ Date: _____

Food diary for today:

Time	Meal	Food	How do you feel?
	Breakfast		
	Morning tea		
	Lunch		
	Afternoon tea		
	Dinner		
	Supper		
	Extra snacks		

Sleep diary:

How many hours?	Quality?	Notes

Rested/tired/restless/interruptions/dreams/thirsty/toilet/worrying/crying?

Exercise diary for today:

Time	Exercise type	How long for?	How do you feel?

Include incidental exercise like climbing stairs, cycling the kids to school or walking to shops.

Mood diary for today:

	6am	8am	10am	12pm	2pm	4pm	6pm	8pm	10 pm	12 am	2am	4am
+5												
+4												
+3												
+2												
+1												
0												
-1												
-2												
-3												
-4												
-5												

Chart your mood with a cross or star either once or over the day.

Social contacts today:

Time	Who did you socialise with? Who are they to you?	How long for?	How do you feel?

Includes contacts at sports/gym, work, home and regular people you see during the day.

How did today go?

_____

_____

_____

What was the worst thing about today? _____

Did you talk with someone about this?   No   Yes

What was the **best thing** about today? _____

Did you talk with someone about this?   No   Yes

_____

"Diamonds are carbon under pressure." Unknown

Month of

January	February	March
April	May	June
July	August	September
October	November	December

Today is _____ Date: _____

Food diary for today:

Time	Meal	Food	How do you feel?
	Breakfast		
	Morning tea		
	Lunch		
	Afternoon tea		
	Dinner		
	Supper		
	Extra snacks		

Sleep diary:

How many hours?	Quality?	Notes

Rested/tired/restless/interruptions/dreams/thirsty/toilet/worrying/crying?

Exercise diary for today:

Time	Exercise type	How long for?	How do you feel?

Include incidental exercise like climbing stairs, cycling the kids to school or walking to shops.

Mood diary for today:

	6am	8am	10am	12pm	2pm	4pm	6pm	8pm	10 pm	12 am	2am	4am
+5												
+4												
+3												
+2												
+1												
0												
-1												
-2												
-3												
-4												
-5												

Chart your mood with a cross or star either once or over the day.

Social contacts today:

Time	Who did you socialise with? Who are they to you?	How long for?	How do you feel?

Includes contacts at sports/gym, work, home and regular people you see during the day.

How did today go?

_____

_____

_____

What was the worst thing about today? _____

Did you talk with someone about this?   No   Yes

What was the **best thing** about today? _____

Did you talk with someone about this?   No   Yes

"Autumn is a second spring, when every leaf is a flower." Albert Camus

Today is _____ Date: _____

Food diary for today:

Time	Meal	Food	How do you feel?
	Breakfast		
	Morning tea		
	Lunch		
	Afternoon tea		
	Dinner		
	Supper		
	Extra snacks		

Sleep diary:

How many hours?	Quality?	Notes

Rested/tired/restless/interruptions/dreams/thirsty/toilet/worrying/crying?

Exercise diary for today:

Time	Exercise type	How long for?	How do you feel?

Include incidental exercise like climbing stairs, cycling the kids to school or walking to shops.

Mood diary for today:

	6am	8am	10am	12pm	2pm	4pm	6pm	8pm	10 pm	12 am	2am	4am
+5												
+4												
+3												
+2												
+1												
0												
-1												
-2												
-3												
-4												
-5												

Chart your mood with a cross or star either once or over the day.

Social contacts today:

Time	Who did you socialise with? Who are they to you?	How long for?	How do you feel?

Includes contacts at sports/gym, work, home and regular people you see during the day.

How did today go?

_____

_____

_____

What was the worst thing about today? _____

Did you talk with someone about this?   No   Yes

What was the **best thing** about today? _____

Did you talk with someone about this?   No   Yes

"Make the best of use of what is in your power and take the rest as it happens" Epictetus

Today is _____ Date: _____

Food diary for today:

Time	Meal	Food	How do you feel?
	Breakfast		
	Morning tea		
	Lunch		
	Afternoon tea		
	Dinner		
	Supper		
	Extra snacks		

Sleep diary:

How many hours?	Quality?	Notes

Rested/tired/restless/interruptions/dreams/thirsty/toilet/worrying/crying?

Exercise diary for today:

Time	Exercise type	How long for?	How do you feel?

Include incidental exercise like climbing stairs, cycling the kids to school or walking to shops.

Mood diary for today:

	6am	8am	10am	12pm	2pm	4pm	6pm	8pm	10 pm	12 am	2am	4am
+5												
+4												
+3												
+2												
+1												
0												
-1												
-2												
-3												
-4												
-5												

Chart your mood with a cross or star either once or over the day.

Social contacts today:

Time	Who did you socialise with? Who are they to you?	How long for?	How do you feel?

Includes contacts at sports/gym, work, home and regular people you see during the day.

How did today go?

_____

_____

_____

What was the worst thing about today? _____

Did you talk with someone about this?   No   Yes

What was the **best thing** about today? _____

Did you talk with someone about this?   No   Yes

"Doubt kills more dreams than failure ever will." Karim Seddiki

Today is _____ Date: _____

Food diary for today:

Time	Meal	Food	How do you feel?
	Breakfast		
	Morning tea		
	Lunch		
	Afternoon tea		
	Dinner		
	Supper		
	Extra snacks		

Sleep diary:

How many hours?	Quality?	Notes

Rested/tired/restless/interruptions/dreams/thirsty/toilet/worrying/crying?

Exercise diary for today:

Time	Exercise type	How long for?	How do you feel?

Include incidental exercise like climbing stairs, cycling the kids to school or walking to shops.

Mood diary for today:

	6am	8am	10am	12pm	2pm	4pm	6pm	8pm	10 pm	12 am	2am	4am
+5												
+4												
+3												
+2												
+1												
0												
-1												
-2												
-3												
-4												
-5												

Chart your mood with a cross or star either once or over the day.

Social contacts today:

Time	Who did you socialise with? Who are they to you?	How long for?	How do you feel?

Includes contacts at sports/gym, work, home and regular people you see during the day.

How did today go?

_____

_____

_____

What was the worst thing about today? _____

Did you talk with someone about this?   No   Yes

What was the **best thing** about today? _____

Did you talk with someone about this?   No   Yes

"Self discipline is doing what needs to be done, even if you don't feel like doing it." Unknown

Today is _____ Date: _____

Food diary for today:

Time	Meal	Food	How do you feel?
	Breakfast		
	Morning tea		
	Lunch		
	Afternoon tea		
	Dinner		
	Supper		
	Extra snacks		

Sleep diary:

How many hours?	Quality?	Notes

Rested/tired/restless/interruptions/dreams/thirsty/toilet/worrying/crying?

Exercise diary for today:

Time	Exercise type	How long for?	How do you feel?

Include incidental exercise like climbing stairs, cycling the kids to school or walking to shops.

Mood diary for today:

	6am	8am	10am	12pm	2pm	4pm	6pm	8pm	10 pm	12 am	2am	4am
+5												
+4												
+3												
+2												
+1												
0												
-1												
-2												
-3												
-4												
-5												

Chart your mood with a cross or star either once or over the day.

Social contacts today:

Time	Who did you socialise with? Who are they to you?	How long for?	How do you feel?

Includes contacts at sports/gym, work, home and regular people you see during the day.

How did today go?

_____

_____

_____

What was the worst thing about today? _____

Did you talk with someone about this?   No   Yes

What was the **best thing** about today? _____

Did you talk with someone about this?   No   Yes

_____

"Smile often, your brain loves it." Chrystal V Benson

Today is _____ Date: _____

Food diary for today:

Time	Meal	Food	How do you feel?
	Breakfast		
	Morning tea		
	Lunch		
	Afternoon tea		
	Dinner		
	Supper		
	Extra snacks		

Sleep diary:

How many hours?	Quality?	Notes

Rested/tired/restless/interruptions/dreams/thirsty/toilet/worrying/crying?

Exercise diary for today:

Time	Exercise type	How long for?	How do you feel?

Include incidental exercise like climbing stairs, cycling the kids to school or walking to shops.

Mood diary for today:

	6am	8am	10am	12pm	2pm	4pm	6pm	8pm	10 pm	12 am	2am	4am
+5												
+4												
+3												
+2												
+1												
0												
-1												
-2												
-3												
-4												
-5												

Chart your mood with a cross or star either once or over the day.

Social contacts today:

Time	Who did you socialise with? Who are they to you?	How long for?	How do you feel?

Includes contacts at sports/gym, work, home and regular people you see during the day.

How did today go?

_____

_____

_____

What was the worst thing about today? _____

Did you talk with someone about this?   No   Yes

What was the **best thing** about today? _____

Did you talk with someone about this?   No   Yes

_____

"Let him that would move the world, first move himself." Socrates

Today is _____ Date: _____

Food diary for today:

Time	Meal	Food	How do you feel?
	Breakfast		
	Morning tea		
	Lunch		
	Afternoon tea		
	Dinner		
	Supper		
	Extra snacks		

Sleep diary:

How many hours?	Quality?	Notes

Rested/tired/restless/interruptions/dreams/thirsty/toilet/worrying/crying?

Exercise diary for today:

Time	Exercise type	How long for?	How do you feel?

Include incidental exercise like climbing stairs, cycling the kids to school or walking to shops.

Mood diary for today:

	6am	8am	10am	12pm	2pm	4pm	6pm	8pm	10 pm	12 am	2am	4am
+5												
+4												
+3												
+2												
+1												
0												
-1												
-2												
-3												
-4												
-5												

Chart your mood with a cross or star either once or over the day.

Social contacts today:

Time	Who did you socialise with? Who are they to you?	How long for?	How do you feel?

Includes contacts at sports/gym, work, home and regular people you see during the day.

How did today go?

_____

_____

_____

What was the worst thing about today? _____

Did you talk with someone about this?   No   Yes

What was the **best thing** about today? _____

Did you talk with someone about this?   No   Yes

"All things are possible, if we believe it so." Unknown

Today is _____ Date: _____

Food diary for today:

Time	Meal	Food	How do you feel?
	Breakfast		
	Morning tea		
	Lunch		
	Afternoon tea		
	Dinner		
	Supper		
	Extra snacks		

Sleep diary:

How many hours?	Quality?	Notes

Rested/tired/restless/interruptions/dreams/thirsty/toilet/worrying/crying?

Exercise diary for today:

Time	Exercise type	How long for?	How do you feel?

Include incidental exercise like climbing stairs, cycling the kids to school or walking to shops.

Mood diary for today:

	6am	8am	10am	12pm	2pm	4pm	6pm	8pm	10 pm	12 am	2am	4am
+5												
+4												
+3												
+2												
+1												
0												
-1												
-2												
-3												
-4												
-5												

Chart your mood with a cross or star either once or over the day.

Social contacts today:

Time	Who did you socialise with? Who are they to you?	How long for?	How do you feel?

Includes contacts at sports/gym, work, home and regular people you see during the day.

How did today go?

_____

_____

_____

What was the worst thing about today? _____

Did you talk with someone about this?   No   Yes

What was the **best thing** about today? _____

Did you talk with someone about this?   No   Yes

"Small deeds done are better than great deeds planned." Unknown

Today is _____ Date: _____

Food diary for today:

Time	Meal	Food	How do you feel?
	Breakfast		
	Morning tea		
	Lunch		
	Afternoon tea		
	Dinner		
	Supper		
	Extra snacks		

Sleep diary:

How many hours?	Quality?	Notes

Rested/tired/restless/interruptions/dreams/thirsty/toilet/worrying/crying?

Exercise diary for today:

Time	Exercise type	How long for?	How do you feel?

Include incidental exercise like climbing stairs, cycling the kids to school or walking to shops.

Mood diary for today:

	6am	8am	10am	12pm	2pm	4pm	6pm	8pm	10 pm	12 am	2am	4am
+5												
+4												
+3												
+2												
+1												
0												
-1												
-2												
-3												
-4												
-5												

Chart your mood with a cross or star either once or over the day.

Social contacts today:

Time	Who did you socialise with? Who are they to you?	How long for?	How do you feel?

Includes contacts at sports/gym, work, home and regular people you see during the day.

How did today go?

_____

_____

_____

What was the worst thing about today? _____

Did you talk with someone about this?   No   Yes

What was the **best thing** about today? _____

Did you talk with someone about this?   No   Yes

_____

"Every day, I am making myself me." Chrystal V Benson

Today is _____ Date: _____

Food diary for today:

Time	Meal	Food	How do you feel?
	Breakfast		
	Morning tea		
	Lunch		
	Afternoon tea		
	Dinner		
	Supper		
	Extra snacks		

Sleep diary:

How many hours?	Quality?	Notes

Rested/tired/restless/interruptions/dreams/thirsty/toilet/worrying/crying?

Exercise diary for today:

Time	Exercise type	How long for?	How do you feel?

Include incidental exercise like climbing stairs, cycling the kids to school or walking to shops.

Mood diary for today:

	6am	8am	10am	12pm	2pm	4pm	6pm	8pm	10 pm	12 am	2am	4am
+5												
+4												
+3												
+2												
+1												
0												
-1												
-2												
-3												
-4												
-5												

Chart your mood with a cross or star either once or over the day.

Social contacts today:

Time	Who did you socialise with? Who are they to you?	How long for?	How do you feel?

Includes contacts at sports/gym, work, home and regular people you see during the day.

How did today go?

_____

_____

_____

What was the worst thing about today? _____

Did you talk with someone about this?   No   Yes

What was the **best thing** about today? _____

Did you talk with someone about this?   No   Yes

"Most things in life are temporary." Ben Franklin

Today is _____ Date: _____

Food diary for today:

Time	Meal	Food	How do you feel?
	Breakfast		
	Morning tea		
	Lunch		
	Afternoon tea		
	Dinner		
	Supper		
	Extra snacks		

Sleep diary:

How many hours?	Quality?	Notes

Rested/tired/restless/interruptions/dreams/thirsty/toilet/worrying/crying?

Exercise diary for today:

Time	Exercise type	How long for?	How do you feel?

Include incidental exercise like climbing stairs, cycling the kids to school or walking to shops.

Mood diary for today:

	6am	8am	10am	12pm	2pm	4pm	6pm	8pm	10 pm	12 am	2am	4am
+5												
+4												
+3												
+2												
+1												
0												
-1												
-2												
-3												
-4												
-5												

Chart your mood with a cross or star either once or over the day.

Social contacts today:

Time	Who did you socialise with? Who are they to you?	How long for?	How do you feel?

Includes contacts at sports/gym, work, home and regular people you see during the day.

How did today go?

_____

_____

_____

What was the worst thing about today? _____

Did you talk with someone about this?   No   Yes

What was the **best thing** about today? _____

Did you talk with someone about this?   No   Yes

_____

"No winter lasts forever and no spring skips its turn." Hal Borland

Today is _____ Date: _____

Food diary for today:

Time	Meal	Food	How do you feel?
	Breakfast		
	Morning tea		
	Lunch		
	Afternoon tea		
	Dinner		
	Supper		
	Extra snacks		

Sleep diary:

How many hours?	Quality?	Notes

Rested/tired/restless/interruptions/dreams/thirsty/toilet/worrying/crying?

Exercise diary for today:

Time	Exercise type	How long for?	How do you feel?

Include incidental exercise like climbing stairs, cycling the kids to school or walking to shops.

Mood diary for today:

	6am	8am	10am	12pm	2pm	4pm	6pm	8pm	10 pm	12 am	2am	4am
+5												
+4												
+3												
+2												
+1												
0												
-1												
-2												
-3												
-4												
-5												

Chart your mood with a cross or star either once or over the day.

Social contacts today:

Time	Who did you socialise with? Who are they to you?	How long for?	How do you feel?

Includes contacts at sports/gym, work, home and regular people you see during the day.

How did today go?

_____

_____

_____

What was the worst thing about today? _____

Did you talk with someone about this?   No   Yes

What was the **best thing** about today? _____

Did you talk with someone about this?   No   Yes

"Men's heart away from nature becomes hard." Standing Bear

Today is _____ Date: _____

Food diary for today:

Time	Meal	Food	How do you feel?
	Breakfast		
	Morning tea		
	Lunch		
	Afternoon tea		
	Dinner		
	Supper		
	Extra snacks		

Sleep diary:

How many hours?	Quality?	Notes

Rested/tired/restless/interruptions/dreams/thirsty/toilet/worrying/crying?

Exercise diary for today:

Time	Exercise type	How long for?	How do you feel?

Include incidental exercise like climbing stairs, cycling the kids to school or walking to shops.

Mood diary for today:

	6am	8am	10am	12pm	2pm	4pm	6pm	8pm	10 pm	12 am	2am	4am
+5												
+4												
+3												
+2												
+1												
0												
-1												
-2												
-3												
-4												
-5												

Chart your mood with a cross or star either once or over the day.

Social contacts today:

Time	Who did you socialise with? Who are they to you?	How long for?	How do you feel?

Includes contacts at sports/gym, work, home and regular people you see during the day.

How did today go?

_____

_____

_____

What was the worst thing about today? _____

Did you talk with someone about this?   No   Yes

What was the **best thing** about today? _____

Did you talk with someone about this?   No   Yes

"Stop thinking too much, sometimes there is no answer and it's okay to not know." Unknown

Today is _____ Date: _____

Food diary for today:

Time	Meal	Food	How do you feel?
	Breakfast		
	Morning tea		
	Lunch		
	Afternoon tea		
	Dinner		
	Supper		
	Extra snacks		

Sleep diary:

How many hours?	Quality?	Notes

Rested/tired/restless/interruptions/dreams/thirsty/toilet/worrying/crying?

Exercise diary for today:

Time	Exercise type	How long for?	How do you feel?

Include incidental exercise like climbing stairs, cycling the kids to school or walking to shops.

Mood diary for today:

	6am	8am	10am	12pm	2pm	4pm	6pm	8pm	10 pm	12 am	2am	4am
+5												
+4												
+3												
+2												
+1												
0												
-1												
-2												
-3												
-4												
-5												

Chart your mood with a cross or star either once or over the day.

Social contacts today:

Time	Who did you socialise with? Who are they to you?	How long for?	How do you feel?

Includes contacts at sports/gym, work, home and regular people you see during the day.

How did today go?

_____

_____

_____

What was the worst thing about today? _____

Did you talk with someone about this?   No   Yes

What was the **best thing** about today? _____

Did you talk with someone about this?   No   Yes

"Know thyself." Gates of Delphi

Today is _____ Date: _____

Food diary for today:

Time	Meal	Food	How do you feel?
	Breakfast		
	Morning tea		
	Lunch		
	Afternoon tea		
	Dinner		
	Supper		
	Extra snacks		

Sleep diary:

How many hours?	Quality?	Notes

Rested/tired/restless/interruptions/dreams/thirsty/toilet/worrying/crying?

Exercise diary for today:

Time	Exercise type	How long for?	How do you feel?

Include incidental exercise like climbing stairs, cycling the kids to school or walking to shops.

Mood diary for today:

	6am	8am	10am	12pm	2pm	4pm	6pm	8pm	10 pm	12 am	2am	4am
+5												
+4												
+3												
+2												
+1												
0												
-1												
-2												
-3												
-4												
-5												

Chart your mood with a cross or star either once or over the day.

Social contacts today:

Time	Who did you socialise with? Who are they to you?	How long for?	How do you feel?

Includes contacts at sports/gym, work, home and regular people you see during the day.

How did today go?

_____

_____

_____

What was the worst thing about today? _____

Did you talk with someone about this?   No   Yes

What was the **best thing** about today? _____

Did you talk with someone about this?   No   Yes

"Your potential grows with each lesson learnt." Unknown

Today is _____ Date: _____

Food diary for today: (include any alcohol intake)

Time	Meal	Food	How do you feel?
	Breakfast		
	Morning tea		
	Lunch		
	Afternoon tea		
	Dinner		
	Supper		
	Extra snacks		

Sleep diary:

How many hours?	Quality?	Notes

Rested/tired/restless/interruptions/dreams/thirsty/toilet/worrying/crying?

Exercise diary for today:

Time	Exercise type	How long for?	How do you feel?

Include incidental exercise like climbing stairs, cycling the kids to school or walking to shops.

Mood diary for today:

	6am	8am	10am	12pm	2pm	4pm	6pm	8pm	10 pm	12 am	2am	4am
+5												
+4												
+3												
+2												
+1												
0												
-1												
-2												
-3												
-4												
-5												

Chart your mood with a cross or star either once or over the day.

Social contacts today:

Time	Who did you socialise with? Who are they to you?	How long for?	How do you feel?

Includes contacts at sports/gym, work, home and regular people you see during the day.

How did today go?

_____

_____

_____

What was the worst thing about today? _____

Did you talk with someone about this?   No   Yes

What was the **best thing** about today? _____

Did you talk with someone about this?   No   Yes

"Some things take time." Unknown

97

Today is _____ Date: _____

Food diary for today: (include any alcohol intake)

Time	Meal	Food	How do you feel?
	Breakfast		
	Morning tea		
	Lunch		
	Afternoon tea		
	Dinner		
	Supper		
	Extra snacks		

Sleep diary:

How many hours?	Quality?	Notes

Rested/tired/restless/interruptions/dreams/thirsty/toilet/worrying/crying?

Exercise diary for today:

Time	Exercise type	How long for?	How do you feel?

Include incidental exercise like climbing stairs, cycling the kids to school or walking to shops.

Mood diary for today:

	6am	8am	10am	12pm	2pm	4pm	6pm	8pm	10 pm	12 am	2am	4am
+5												
+4												
+3												
+2												
+1												
0												
-1												
-2												
-3												
-4												
-5												

Chart your mood with a cross or star either once or over the day.

Social contacts today:

Time	Who did you socialise with? Who are they to you?	How long for?	How do you feel?

Includes contacts at sports/gym, work, home and regular people you see during the day.

How did today go?

_____

_____

_____

What was the worst thing about today? _____

Did you talk with someone about this?   No   Yes

What was the **best thing** about today? _____

Did you talk with someone about this?   No   Yes

_____

"I have never met a strong person with an easy past." Atticus

Today is _____ Date: _____

Food diary for today: (include any alcohol intake)

Time	Meal	Food	How do you feel?
	Breakfast		
	Morning tea		
	Lunch		
	Afternoon tea		
	Dinner		
	Supper		
	Extra snacks		

Sleep diary:

How many hours?	Quality?	Notes

Rested/tired/restless/interruptions/dreams/thirsty/toilet/worrying/crying?

Exercise diary for today:

Time	Exercise type	How long for?	How do you feel?

Include incidental exercise like climbing stairs, cycling the kids to school or walking to shops.

Mood diary for today:

	6am	8am	10am	12pm	2pm	4pm	6pm	8pm	10 pm	12 am	2am	4am
+5												
+4												
+3												
+2												
+1												
0												
-1												
-2												
-3												
-4												
-5												

Chart your mood with a cross or star either once or over the day.

Social contacts today:

Time	Who did you socialise with? Who are they to you?	How long for?	How do you feel?

Includes contacts at sports/gym, work, home and regular people you see during the day.

How did today go?

_____

_____

_____

What was the worst thing about today? _____

Did you talk with someone about this?   No   Yes

What was the **best thing** about today? _____

Did you talk with someone about this?   No   Yes

"What you tell yourself everyday will either lift you up, or drag you down, you choose." Unknown

Today is _____ Date: _____

Food diary for today: (include any alcohol intake)

Time	Meal	Food	How do you feel?
	Breakfast		
	Morning tea		
	Lunch		
	Afternoon tea		
	Dinner		
	Supper		
	Extra snacks		

Sleep diary:

How many hours?	Quality?	Notes

Rested/tired/restless/interruptions/dreams/thirsty/toilet/worrying/crying?

Exercise diary for today:

Time	Exercise type	How long for?	How do you feel?

Include incidental exercise like climbing stairs, cycling the kids to school or walking to shops.

Mood diary for today:

	6am	8am	10am	12pm	2pm	4pm	6pm	8pm	10 pm	12 am	2am	4am
+5												
+4												
+3												
+2												
+1												
0												
-1												
-2												
-3												
-4												
-5												

Chart your mood with a cross or star either once or over the day.

Social contacts today:

Time	Who did you socialise with? Who are they to you?	How long for?	How do you feel?

Includes contacts at sports/gym, work, home and regular people you see during the day.

How did today go?

_____

_____

_____

What was the worst thing about today? _____

Did you talk with someone about this?   No   Yes

What was the **best thing** about today? _____

Did you talk with someone about this?   No   Yes

_____

"Why limit happy to an hour." WC Fields

Today is _____ Date: _____

Food diary for today: (include any alcohol intake)

Time	Meal	Food	How do you feel?
	Breakfast		
	Morning tea		
	Lunch		
	Afternoon tea		
	Dinner		
	Supper		
	Extra snacks		

Sleep diary:

How many hours?	Quality?	Notes

Rested/tired/restless/interruptions/dreams/thirsty/toilet/worrying/crying?

Exercise diary for today:

Time	Exercise type	How long for?	How do you feel?

Include incidental exercise like climbing stairs, cycling the kids to school or walking to shops.

Mood diary for today:

	6am	8am	10am	12pm	2pm	4pm	6pm	8pm	10 pm	12 am	2am	4am
+5												
+4												
+3												
+2												
+1												
0												
-1												
-2												
-3												
-4												
-5												

Chart your mood with a cross or star either once or over the day.

Social contacts today:

Time	Who did you socialise with? Who are they to you?	How long for?	How do you feel?

Includes contacts at sports/gym, work, home and regular people you see during the day.

How did today go?

_____

_____

_____

What was the worst thing about today? _____

Did you talk with someone about this?   No   Yes

What was the **best thing** about today? _____

Did you talk with someone about this?   No   Yes

"No matter how you feel, if you really need to, get up, get dressed and show up, you'll feel better for it." Unknown

Today is _____ Date: _____

Food diary for today: (include any alcohol intake)

Time	Meal	Food	How do you feel?
	Breakfast		
	Morning tea		
	Lunch		
	Afternoon tea		
	Dinner		
	Supper		
	Extra snacks		

Sleep diary:

How many hours?	Quality?	Notes

Rested/tired/restless/interruptions/dreams/thirsty/toilet/worrying/crying?

Exercise diary for today:

Time	Exercise type	How long for?	How do you feel?

Include incidental exercise like climbing stairs, cycling the kids to school or walking to shops.

Mood diary for today:

	6am	8am	10am	12pm	2pm	4pm	6pm	8pm	10 pm	12 am	2am	4am
+5												
+4												
+3												
+2												
+1												
0												
-1												
-2												
-3												
-4												
-5												

Chart your mood with a cross or star either once or over the day.

Social contacts today:

Time	Who did you socialise with? Who are they to you?	How long for?	How do you feel?

Includes contacts at sports/gym, work, home and regular people you see during the day.

How did today go?

_____

_____

_____

What was the worst thing about today? _____

Did you talk with someone about this?   No   Yes

What was the **best thing** about today? _____

Did you talk with someone about this?   No   Yes

_____

"I fight for my health everyday. I am not lazy. I am a warrior." Unknown

Today is _____ Date: _____

Food diary for today: (include any alcohol intake)

Time	Meal	Food	How do you feel?
	Breakfast		
	Morning tea		
	Lunch		
	Afternoon tea		
	Dinner		
	Supper		
	Extra snacks		

Sleep diary:

How many hours?	Quality?	Notes

Rested/tired/restless/interruptions/dreams/thirsty/toilet/worrying/crying?

Exercise diary for today:

Time	Exercise type	How long for?	How do you feel?

Include incidental exercise like climbing stairs, cycling the kids to school or walking to shops.

Mood diary for today:

	6am	8am	10am	12pm	2pm	4pm	6pm	8pm	10 pm	12 am	2am	4am
+5												
+4												
+3												
+2												
+1												
0												
-1												
-2												
-3												
-4												
-5												

Chart your mood with a cross or star either once or over the day.

Social contacts today:

Time	Who did you socialise with? Who are they to you?	How long for?	How do you feel?

Includes contacts at sports/gym, work, home and regular people you see during the day.

How did today go?

_____

_____

_____

What was the worst thing about today? _____

Did you talk with someone about this?   No   Yes

What was the **best thing** about today? _____

Did you talk with someone about this?   No   Yes

_____

"Self-forgiveness is essential for self-healing." Unknown

Today is _____ Date: _____

Food diary for today: (include any alcohol intake)

Time	Meal	Food	How do you feel?
	Breakfast		
	Morning tea		
	Lunch		
	Afternoon tea		
	Dinner		
	Supper		
	Extra snacks		

Sleep diary:

How many hours?	Quality?	Notes

Rested/tired/restless/interruptions/dreams/thirsty/toilet/worrying/crying?

Exercise diary for today:

Time	Exercise type	How long for?	How do you feel?

Include incidental exercise like climbing stairs, cycling the kids to school or walking to shops.

Mood diary for today:

	6am	8am	10am	12pm	2pm	4pm	6pm	8pm	10 pm	12 am	2am	4am
+5												
+4												
+3												
+2												
+1												
0												
-1												
-2												
-3												
-4												
-5												

Chart your mood with a cross or star either once or over the day.

Social contacts today:

Time	Who did you socialise with? Who are they to you?	How long for?	How do you feel?

Includes contacts at sports/gym, work, home and regular people you see during the day.

How did today go?

_____

_____

_____

What was the worst thing about today? _____

Did you talk with someone about this?   No   Yes

What was the **best thing** about today? _____

Did you talk with someone about this?   No   Yes

"The weak can never forgive, forgiveness is the attribute of the strong." Mahatma Ghandi

Today is _____ Date: _____

Food diary for today: (include any alcohol intake)

Time	Meal	Food	How do you feel?
	Breakfast		
	Morning tea		
	Lunch		
	Afternoon tea		
	Dinner		
	Supper		
	Extra snacks		

Sleep diary:

How many hours?	Quality?	Notes

Rested/tired/restless/interruptions/dreams/thirsty/toilet/worrying/crying?

Exercise diary for today:

Time	Exercise type	How long for?	How do you feel?

Include incidental exercise like climbing stairs, cycling the kids to school or walking to shops.

Mood diary for today:

	6am	8am	10am	12pm	2pm	4pm	6pm	8pm	10 pm	12 am	2am	4am
+5												
+4												
+3												
+2												
+1												
0												
-1												
-2												
-3												
-4												
-5												

Chart your mood with a cross or star either once or over the day.

Social contacts today:

Time	Who did you socialise with? Who are they to you?	How long for?	How do you feel?

Includes contacts at sports/gym, work, home and regular people you see during the day.

How did today go?

_____

_____

_____

What was the worst thing about today? _____

Did you talk with someone about this?   No   Yes

What was the **best thing** about today? _____

Did you talk with someone about this?   No   Yes

"Found your tribe yet?" Unknown

113

Today is _____ Date: _____

Food diary for today: (include any alcohol intake)

Time	Meal	Food	How do you feel?
	Breakfast		
	Morning tea		
	Lunch		
	Afternoon tea		
	Dinner		
	Supper		
	Extra snacks		

Sleep diary:

How many hours?	Quality?	Notes

Rested/tired/restless/interruptions/dreams/thirsty/toilet/worrying/crying?

Exercise diary for today:

Time	Exercise type	How long for?	How do you feel?

Include incidental exercise like climbing stairs, cycling the kids to school or walking to shops.

Mood diary for today:

	6am	8am	10am	12pm	2pm	4pm	6pm	8pm	10 pm	12 am	2am	4am
+5												
+4												
+3												
+2												
+1												
0												
-1												
-2												
-3												
-4												
-5												

Chart your mood with a cross or star either once or over the day.

Social contacts today:

Time	Who did you socialise with? Who are they to you?	How long for?	How do you feel?

Includes contacts at sports/gym, work, home and regular people you see during the day.

How did today go?

_____

_____

_____

What was the worst thing about today? _____

Did you talk with someone about this?   No   Yes

What was the **best thing** about today? _____

Did you talk with someone about this?   No   Yes

_____

"Pain is real, so is hope." Unknown

Today is _____ Date: _____

Food diary for today: (include any alcohol intake)

Time	Meal	Food	How do you feel?
	Breakfast		
	Morning tea		
	Lunch		
	Afternoon tea		
	Dinner		
	Supper		
	Extra snacks		

Sleep diary:

How many hours?	Quality?	Notes

Rested/tired/restless/interruptions/dreams/thirsty/toilet/worrying/crying?

Exercise diary for today:

Time	Exercise type	How long for?	How do you feel?

Include incidental exercise like climbing stairs, cycling the kids to school or walking to shops.

Mood diary for today:

	6am	8am	10am	12pm	2pm	4pm	6pm	8pm	10 pm	12 am	2am	4am
+5												
+4												
+3												
+2												
+1												
0												
-1												
-2												
-3												
-4												
-5												

Chart your mood with a cross or star either once or over the day.

Social contacts today:

Time	Who did you socialise with? Who are they to you?	How long for?	How do you feel?

Includes contacts at sports/gym, work, home and regular people you see during the day.

How did today go?

_____

_____

_____

What was the worst thing about today? _____

Did you talk with someone about this?   No   Yes

What was the **best thing** about today? _____

Did you talk with someone about this?   No   Yes

"I myself, am made of flaws, stitched together with good intentions." Augusten Burroughs

Today is _____ Date: _____

Food diary for today: (include any alcohol intake)

Time	Meal	Food	How do you feel?
	Breakfast		
	Morning tea		
	Lunch		
	Afternoon tea		
	Dinner		
	Supper		
	Extra snacks		

Sleep diary:

How many hours?	Quality?	Notes

Rested/tired/restless/interruptions/dreams/thirsty/toilet/worrying/crying?

Exercise diary for today:

Time	Exercise type	How long for?	How do you feel?

Include incidental exercise like climbing stairs, cycling the kids to school or walking to shops.

Mood diary for today:

	6am	8am	10am	12pm	2pm	4pm	6pm	8pm	10 pm	12 am	2am	4am
+5												
+4												
+3												
+2												
+1												
0												
-1												
-2												
-3												
-4												
-5												

Chart your mood with a cross or star either once or over the day.

Social contacts today:

Time	Who did you socialise with? Who are they to you?	How long for?	How do you feel?

Includes contacts at sports/gym, work, home and regular people you see during the day.

How did today go?

_____

_____

_____

What was the worst thing about today? _____

Did you talk with someone about this?   No   Yes

What was the **best thing** about today? _____

Did you talk with someone about this?   No   Yes

"Your opinion of me doesn't determine who I am." Unknown

Today is _____ Date: _____

Food diary for today: (include any alcohol intake)

Time	Meal	Food	How do you feel?
	Breakfast		
	Morning tea		
	Lunch		
	Afternoon tea		
	Dinner		
	Supper		
	Extra snacks		

Sleep diary:

How many hours?	Quality?	Notes

Rested/tired/restless/interruptions/dreams/thirsty/toilet/worrying/crying?

Exercise diary for today:

Time	Exercise type	How long for?	How do you feel?

Include incidental exercise like climbing stairs, cycling the kids to school or walking to shops.

Mood diary for today:

	6am	8am	10am	12pm	2pm	4pm	6pm	8pm	10 pm	12 am	2am	4am
+5												
+4												
+3												
+2												
+1												
0												
-1												
-2												
-3												
-4												
-5												

Chart your mood with a cross or star either once or over the day.

Social contacts today:

Time	Who did you socialise with? Who are they to you?	How long for?	How do you feel?

Includes contacts at sports/gym, work, home and regular people you see during the day.

How did today go?

_____

_____

_____

What was the worst thing about today? _____

Did you talk with someone about this?   No   Yes

What was the **best thing** about today? _____

Did you talk with someone about this?   No   Yes

*"How much is in your emotional tank today?
Do you need a refill?" Unknown*

Today is _____ Date: _____

Food diary for today: (include any alcohol intake)

Time	Meal	Food	How do you feel?
	Breakfast		
	Morning tea		
	Lunch		
	Afternoon tea		
	Dinner		
	Supper		
	Extra snacks		

Sleep diary:

How many hours?	Quality?	Notes

Rested/tired/restless/interruptions/dreams/thirsty/toilet/worrying/crying?

Exercise diary for today:

Time	Exercise type	How long for?	How do you feel?

Include incidental exercise like climbing stairs, cycling the kids to school or walking to shops.

Mood diary for today:

	6am	8am	10am	12pm	2pm	4pm	6pm	8pm	10 pm	12 am	2am	4am
+5												
+4												
+3												
+2												
+1												
0												
-1												
-2												
-3												
-4												
-5												

Chart your mood with a cross or star either once or over the day.

Social contacts today:

Time	Who did you socialise with? Who are they to you?	How long for?	How do you feel?

Includes contacts at sports/gym, work, home and regular people you see during the day.

How did today go?

_____

_____

_____

What was the worst thing about today? _____

Did you talk with someone about this?   No   Yes

What was the **best thing** about today? _____

Did you talk with someone about this?   No   Yes

"The greatest need of humans is to be connected and appreciated." Unknown

Month of

January	February	March
April	May	June
July	August	September
October	November	December

Today is _____ Date: _____

Food diary for today: (include any alcohol intake)

Time	Meal	Food	How do you feel?
	Breakfast		
	Morning tea		
	Lunch		
	Afternoon tea		
	Dinner		
	Supper		
	Extra snacks		

Sleep diary:

How many hours?	Quality?	Notes

Rested/tired/restless/interruptions/dreams/thirsty/toilet/worrying/crying?

Exercise diary for today:

Time	Exercise type	How long for?	How do you feel?

Include incidental exercise like climbing stairs, cycling the kids to school or walking to shops.

Mood diary for today:

	6am	8am	10am	12pm	2pm	4pm	6pm	8pm	10 pm	12 am	2am	4am
+5												
+4												
+3												
+2												
+1												
0												
-1												
-2												
-3												
-4												
-5												

Chart your mood with a cross or star either once or over the day.

Social contacts today:

Time	Who did you socialise with? Who are they to you?	How long for?	How do you feel?

Includes contacts at sports/gym, work, home and regular people you see during the day.

How did today go?

_____

_____

_____

What was the worst thing about today? _____

Did you talk with someone about this?   No   Yes

What was the **best thing** about today? _____

Did you talk with someone about this?   No   Yes

"Take a moment, compliment another and everybody feels joy."
Chrystal V Benson

Today is _____ Date: _____

Food diary for today: (include any alcohol intake)

Time	Meal	Food	How do you feel?
	Breakfast		
	Morning tea		
	Lunch		
	Afternoon tea		
	Dinner		
	Supper		
	Extra snacks		

Sleep diary:

How many hours?	Quality?	Notes

Rested/tired/restless/interruptions/dreams/thirsty/toilet/worrying/crying?

Exercise diary for today:

Time	Exercise type	How long for?	How do you feel?

Include incidental exercise like climbing stairs, cycling the kids to school or walking to shops.

Mood diary for today:

	6am	8am	10am	12pm	2pm	4pm	6pm	8pm	10 pm	12 am	2am	4am
+5												
+4												
+3												
+2												
+1												
0												
-1												
-2												
-3												
-4												
-5												

Chart your mood with a cross or star either once or over the day.

Social contacts today:

Time	Who did you socialise with? Who are they to you?	How long for?	How do you feel?

Includes contacts at sports/gym, work, home and regular people you see during the day.

How did today go?

_____

_____

_____

What was the worst thing about today? _____

Did you talk with someone about this?   No   Yes

What was the **best thing** about today? _____

Did you talk with someone about this?   No   Yes

"Style comes in all shapes and sizes. Therefore, the bigger you are, the more style you have." Miss Piggy

Today is _____ Date: _____

Food diary for today: (include any alcohol intake)

Time	Meal	Food	How do you feel?
	Breakfast		
	Morning tea		
	Lunch		
	Afternoon tea		
	Dinner		
	Supper		
	Extra snacks		

Sleep diary:

How many hours?	Quality?	Notes

Rested/tired/restless/interruptions/dreams/thirsty/toilet/worrying/crying?

Exercise diary for today:

Time	Exercise type	How long for?	How do you feel?

Include incidental exercise like climbing stairs, cycling the kids to school or walking to shops.

Mood diary for today:

	6am	8am	10am	12pm	2pm	4pm	6pm	8pm	10 pm	12 am	2am	4am
+5												
+4												
+3												
+2												
+1												
0												
-1												
-2												
-3												
-4												
-5												

Chart your mood with a cross or star either once or over the day.

Social contacts today:

Time	Who did you socialise with? Who are they to you?	How long for?	How do you feel?

Includes contacts at sports/gym, work, home and regular people you see during the day.

How did today go?

_____

_____

_____

What was the worst thing about today? _____

Did you talk with someone about this?   No   Yes

What was the **best thing** about today? _____

Did you talk with someone about this?   No   Yes

"The best way out is always through." Robert Frost

Today is _____ Date: _____

Food diary for today: (include any alcohol intake)

Time	Meal	Food	How do you feel?
	Breakfast		
	Morning tea		
	Lunch		
	Afternoon tea		
	Dinner		
	Supper		
	Extra snacks		

Sleep diary:

How many hours?	Quality?	Notes

Rested/tired/restless/interruptions/dreams/thirsty/toilet/worrying/crying?

Exercise diary for today:

Time	Exercise type	How long for?	How do you feel?

Include incidental exercise like climbing stairs, cycling the kids to school or walking to shops.

Mood diary for today:

	6am	8am	10am	12pm	2pm	4pm	6pm	8pm	10 pm	12 am	2am	4am
+5												
+4												
+3												
+2												
+1												
0												
-1												
-2												
-3												
-4												
-5												

Chart your mood with a cross or star either once or over the day.

Social contacts today:

Time	Who did you socialise with? Who are they to you?	How long for?	How do you feel?

Includes contacts at sports/gym, work, home and regular people you see during the day.

How did today go?

_____

_____

_____

What was the worst thing about today? _____

Did you talk with someone about this?   No   Yes

What was the **best thing** about today? _____

Did you talk with someone about this?   No   Yes

"The flower that blooms in adversity is the rarest and most beautiful of all." Mulan

Today is _____ Date: _____

Food diary for today: (include any alcohol intake)

Time	Meal	Food	How do you feel?
	Breakfast		
	Morning tea		
	Lunch		
	Afternoon tea		
	Dinner		
	Supper		
	Extra snacks		

Sleep diary:

How many hours?	Quality?	Notes

Rested/tired/restless/interruptions/dreams/thirsty/toilet/worrying/crying?

Exercise diary for today:

Time	Exercise type	How long for?	How do you feel?

Include incidental exercise like climbing stairs, cycling the kids to school or walking to shops.

Mood diary for today:

	6am	8am	10am	12pm	2pm	4pm	6pm	8pm	10 pm	12 am	2am	4am
+5												
+4												
+3												
+2												
+1												
0												
-1												
-2												
-3												
-4												
-5												

Chart your mood with a cross or star either once or over the day.

Social contacts today:

Time	Who did you socialise with? Who are they to you?	How long for?	How do you feel?

Includes contacts at sports/gym, work, home and regular people you see during the day.

How did today go?

_____

_____

_____

What was the worst thing about today? _____

Did you talk with someone about this?   No   Yes

What was the **best thing** about today? _____

Did you talk with someone about this?   No   Yes

"It is never too late to be who you might have been." George Elliot

Today is _____ Date: _____

Food diary for today: (include any alcohol intake)

Time	Meal	Food	How do you feel?
	Breakfast		
	Morning tea		
	Lunch		
	Afternoon tea		
	Dinner		
	Supper		
	Extra snacks		

Sleep diary:

How many hours?	Quality?	Notes

Rested/tired/restless/interruptions/dreams/thirsty/toilet/worrying/crying?

Exercise diary for today:

Time	Exercise type	How long for?	How do you feel?

Include incidental exercise like climbing stairs, cycling the kids to school or walking to shops.

Mood diary for today:

	6am	8am	10am	12pm	2pm	4pm	6pm	8pm	10 pm	12 am	2am	4am
+5												
+4												
+3												
+2												
+1												
0												
-1												
-2												
-3												
-4												
-5												

Chart your mood with a cross or star either once or over the day.

Social contacts today:

Time	Who did you socialise with? Who are they to you?	How long for?	How do you feel?

Includes contacts at sports/gym, work, home and regular people you see during the day.

How did today go?

_____

_____

_____

What was the worst thing about today? _____

Did you talk with someone about this?   No   Yes

What was the **best thing** about today? _____

Did you talk with someone about this?   No   Yes

"What lies behind us and what lies before us are tiny matters compared to what lies within us." Ralph Waldo Emerson

Today is _____ Date: _____

Food diary for today: (include any alcohol intake)

Time	Meal	Food	How do you feel?
	Breakfast		
	Morning tea		
	Lunch		
	Afternoon tea		
	Dinner		
	Supper		
	Extra snacks		

Sleep diary:

How many hours?	Quality?	Notes
	.	

Rested/tired/restless/interruptions/dreams/thirsty/toilet/worrying/crying?

Exercise diary for today:

Time	Exercise type	How long for?	How do you feel?

Include incidental exercise like climbing stairs, cycling the kids to school or walking to shops.

Mood diary for today:

	6am	8am	10am	12pm	2pm	4pm	6pm	8pm	10 pm	12 am	2am	4am
+5												
+4												
+3												
+2												
+1												
0												
-1												
-2												
-3												
-4												
-5												

Chart your mood with a cross or star either once or over the day.

Social contacts today:

Time	Who did you socialise with? Who are they to you?	How long for?	How do you feel?

Includes contacts at sports/gym, work, home and regular people you see during the day.

How did today go?

_____

_____

_____

What was the worst thing about today? _____

Did you talk with someone about this?   No   Yes

What was the **best thing** about today? _____

Did you talk with someone about this?   No   Yes

"Make peace with your past, over time it moves beyond the horizon and you miss the opportunity." Unknown

Today is _____ Date: _____

Food diary for today: (include any alcohol intake)

Time	Meal	Food	How do you feel?
	Breakfast		
	Morning tea		
	Lunch		
	Afternoon tea		
	Dinner		
	Supper		
	Extra snacks		

Sleep diary:

How many hours?	Quality?	Notes

Rested/tired/restless/interruptions/dreams/thirsty/toilet/worrying/crying?

Exercise diary for today:

Time	Exercise type	How long for?	How do you feel?

Include incidental exercise like climbing stairs, cycling the kids to school or walking to shops.

Mood diary for today:

	6am	8am	10am	12pm	2pm	4pm	6pm	8pm	10 pm	12 am	2am	4am
+5												
+4												
+3												
+2												
+1												
0												
-1												
-2												
-3												
-4												
-5												

Chart your mood with a cross or star either once or over the day.

Social contacts today:

Time	Who did you socialise with? Who are they to you?	How long for?	How do you feel?

Includes contacts at sports/gym, work, home and regular people you see during the day.

How did today go?

_____

_____

_____

What was the worst thing about today? _____

Did you talk with someone about this?   No   Yes

What was the **best thing** about today? _____

Did you talk with someone about this?   No   Yes

"Let us not be too particular. It is better to have second
hand diamonds than none at all." Mark Twain

Today is _____ Date: _____

Food diary for today: (include any alcohol intake)

Time	Meal	Food	How do you feel?
	Breakfast		
	Morning tea		
	Lunch		
	Afternoon tea		
	Dinner		
	Supper		
	Extra snacks		

Sleep diary:

How many hours?	Quality?	Notes

Rested/tired/restless/interruptions/dreams/thirsty/toilet/worrying/crying?

Exercise diary for today:

Time	Exercise type	How long for?	How do you feel?

Include incidental exercise like climbing stairs, cycling the kids to school or walking to shops.

Mood diary for today:

	6am	8am	10am	12pm	2pm	4pm	6pm	8pm	10 pm	12 am	2am	4am
+5												
+4												
+3												
+2												
+1												
0												
-1												
-2												
-3												
-4												
-5												

Chart your mood with a cross or star either once or over the day.

Social contacts today:

Time	Who did you socialise with? Who are they to you?	How long for?	How do you feel?

Includes contacts at sports/gym, work, home and regular people you see during the day.

How did today go?

_____

_____

_____

What was the worst thing about today? _____

Did you talk with someone about this?   No   Yes

What was the **best thing** about today? _____

Did you talk with someone about this?   No   Yes

_____

"The greatest griefs are the ones we cause ourselves. Be kind to yourself, you're a new design model and testing it out." Unknown

Today is _____ Date: _____

Food diary for today: (include any alcohol intake)

Time	Meal	Food	How do you feel?
	Breakfast		
	Morning tea		
	Lunch		
	Afternoon tea		
	Dinner		
	Supper		
	Extra snacks		

Sleep diary:

How many hours?	Quality?	Notes

Rested/tired/restless/interruptions/dreams/thirsty/toilet/worrying/crying?

Exercise diary for today:

Time	Exercise type	How long for?	How do you feel?

Include incidental exercise like climbing stairs, cycling the kids to school or walking to shops.

Mood diary for today:

	6am	8am	10am	12pm	2pm	4pm	6pm	8pm	10 pm	12 am	2am	4am
+5												
+4												
+3												
+2												
+1												
0												
-1												
-2												
-3												
-4												
-5												

Chart your mood with a cross or star either once or over the day.

Social contacts today:

Time	Who did you socialise with? Who are they to you?	How long for?	How do you feel?

Includes contacts at sports/gym, work, home and regular people you see during the day.

How did today go?

_____

_____

_____

What was the worst thing about today? _____

Did you talk with someone about this?   No   Yes

What was the **best thing** about today? _____

Did you talk with someone about this?   No   Yes

"To thine own self be true". Hamlet - William Shakespeare

Today is _____ Date: _____

Food diary for today: (include any alcohol intake)

Time	Meal	Food	How do you feel?
	Breakfast		
	Morning tea		
	Lunch		
	Afternoon tea		
	Dinner		
	Supper		
	Extra snacks		

Sleep diary:

How many hours?	Quality?	Notes

Rested/tired/restless/interruptions/dreams/thirsty/toilet/worrying/crying?

Exercise diary for today:

Time	Exercise type	How long for?	How do you feel?

Include incidental exercise like climbing stairs, cycling the kids to school or walking to shops.

Mood diary for today:

	6am	8am	10am	12pm	2pm	4pm	6pm	8pm	10 pm	12 am	2am	4am
+5												
+4												
+3												
+2												
+1												
0												
-1												
-2												
-3												
-4												
-5												

Chart your mood with a cross or star either once or over the day.

Social contacts today:

Time	Who did you socialise with? Who are they to you?	How long for?	How do you feel?

Includes contacts at sports/gym, work, home and regular people you see during the day.

How did today go?

_____

_____

_____

What was the worst thing about today? _____

Did you talk with someone about this?   No   Yes

What was the **best thing** about today? _____

Did you talk with someone about this?   No   Yes

_____

"Will it be easy? Nope. Will it be worth it? Yep! Absolutely." Unknown

Today is _____ Date: _____

Food diary for today: (include any alcohol intake)

Time	Meal	Food	How do you feel?
	Breakfast		
	Morning tea		
	Lunch		
	Afternoon tea		
	Dinner		
	Supper		
	Extra snacks		

Sleep diary:

How many hours?	Quality?	Notes

Rested/tired/restless/interruptions/dreams/thirsty/toilet/worrying/crying?

Exercise diary for today:

Time	Exercise type	How long for?	How do you feel?

Include incidental exercise like climbing stairs, cycling the kids to school or walking to shops.

Mood diary for today:

	6am	8am	10am	12pm	2pm	4pm	6pm	8pm	10 pm	12 am	2am	4am
+5												
+4												
+3												
+2												
+1												
0												
-1												
-2												
-3												
-4												
-5												

Chart your mood with a cross or star either once or over the day.

Social contacts today:

Time	Who did you socialise with? Who are they to you?	How long for?	How do you feel?

Includes contacts at sports/gym, work, home and regular people you see during the day.

How did today go?

_____

_____

_____

What was the worst thing about today? _____

Did you talk with someone about this?   No   Yes

What was the **best thing** about today? _____

Did you talk with someone about this?   No   Yes

_____

"Beware permanent decisions to temporary problems." Unknown

Today is _____ Date: _____

Food diary for today: (include any alcohol intake)

Time	Meal	Food	How do you feel?
	Breakfast		
	Morning tea		
	Lunch		
	Afternoon tea		
	Dinner		
	Supper		
	Extra snacks		

Sleep diary:

How many hours?	Quality?	Notes

Rested/tired/restless/interruptions/dreams/thirsty/toilet/worrying/crying?

Exercise diary for today:

Time	Exercise type	How long for?	How do you feel?

Include incidental exercise like climbing stairs, cycling the kids to school or walking to shops.

Mood diary for today:

	6am	8am	10am	12pm	2pm	4pm	6pm	8pm	10 pm	12 am	2am	4am
+5												
+4												
+3												
+2												
+1												
0												
-1												
-2												
-3												
-4												
-5												

Chart your mood with a cross or star either once or over the day.

Social contacts today:

Time	Who did you socialise with? Who are they to you?	How long for?	How do you feel?

Includes contacts at sports/gym, work, home and regular people you see during the day.

How did today go?

_____

_____

_____

What was the worst thing about today? _____

Did you talk with someone about this?   No   Yes

What was the **best thing** about today? _____

Did you talk with someone about this?   No   Yes

_____

"There is a lot of good to life. Stay focused on this gift so you can appreciate it." Unknown

Today is _____ Date: _____

Food diary for today: (include any alcohol intake)

Time	Meal	Food	How do you feel?
	Breakfast		
	Morning tea		
	Lunch		
	Afternoon tea		
	Dinner		
	Supper		
	Extra snacks		

Sleep diary:

How many hours?	Quality?	Notes

Rested/tired/restless/interruptions/dreams/thirsty/toilet/worrying/crying?

Exercise diary for today:

Time	Exercise type	How long for?	How do you feel?

Include incidental exercise like climbing stairs, cycling the kids to school or walking to shops.

Mood diary for today:

	6am	8am	10am	12pm	2pm	4pm	6pm	8pm	10 pm	12 am	2am	4am
+5												
+4												
+3												
+2												
+1												
0												
-1												
-2												
-3												
-4												
-5												

Chart your mood with a cross or star either once or over the day.

Social contacts today:

Time	Who did you socialise with? Who are they to you?	How long for?	How do you feel?

Includes contacts at sports/gym, work, home and regular people you see during the day.

How did today go?

_____

_____

_____

What was the worst thing about today? _____

Did you talk with someone about this?   No   Yes

What was the **best thing** about today? _____

Did you talk with someone about this?   No   Yes

"There is nothing either good or bad, but thinking makes it so." Hamlet - William Shakespeare

Today is _____ Date: _____

Food diary for today: (include any alcohol intake)

Time	Meal	Food	How do you feel?
	Breakfast		
	Morning tea		
	Lunch		
	Afternoon tea		
	Dinner		
	Supper		
	Extra snacks		

Sleep diary:

How many hours?	Quality?	Notes

Rested/tired/restless/interruptions/dreams/thirsty/toilet/worrying/crying?

Exercise diary for today:

Time	Exercise type	How long for?	How do you feel?

Include incidental exercise like climbing stairs, cycling the kids to school or walking to shops.

Mood diary for today:

	6am	8am	10am	12pm	2pm	4pm	6pm	8pm	10 pm	12 am	2am	4am
+5												
+4												
+3												
+2												
+1												
0												
-1												
-2												
-3												
-4												
-5												

Chart your mood with a cross or star either once or over the day.

Social contacts today:

Time	Who did you socialise with? Who are they to you?	How long for?	How do you feel?

Includes contacts at sports/gym, work, home and regular people you see during the day.

How did today go?

_____

_____

_____

What was the worst thing about today? _____

Did you talk with someone about this?   No   Yes

What was the **best thing** about today? _____

Did you talk with someone about this?   No   Yes

"Whether you think you can or think you can't, you are right." Henry Ford

Today is _____ Date: _____

Food diary for today: (include any alcohol intake)

Time	Meal	Food	How do you feel?
	Breakfast		
	Morning tea		
	Lunch		
	Afternoon tea		
	Dinner		
	Supper		
	Extra snacks		

Sleep diary:

How many hours?	Quality?	Notes

Rested/tired/restless/interruptions/dreams/thirsty/toilet/worrying/crying?

Exercise diary for today:

Time	Exercise type	How long for?	How do you feel?

Include incidental exercise like climbing stairs, cycling the kids to school or walking to shops.

Mood diary for today:

	6am	8am	10am	12pm	2pm	4pm	6pm	8pm	10 pm	12 am	2am	4am
+5												
+4												
+3												
+2												
+1												
0												
-1												
-2												
-3												
-4												
-5												

Chart your mood with a cross or star either once or over the day.

Social contacts today:

Time	Who did you socialise with? Who are they to you?	How long for?	How do you feel?

Includes contacts at sports/gym, work, home and regular people you see during the day.

How did today go?

_____

_____

_____

What was the worst thing about today? _____

Did you talk with someone about this?   No   Yes

What was the **best thing** about today? _____

Did you talk with someone about this?   No   Yes

"Sometimes, that's good enough for now." Chrystal V Benson

Today is _____ Date: _____

Food diary for today: (include any alcohol intake)

Time	Meal	Food	How do you feel?
	Breakfast		
	Morning tea		
	Lunch		
	Afternoon tea		
	Dinner		
	Supper		
	Extra snacks		

Sleep diary:

How many hours?	Quality?	Notes

Rested/tired/restless/interruptions/dreams/thirsty/toilet/worrying/crying?

Exercise diary for today:

Time	Exercise type	How long for?	How do you feel?

Include incidental exercise like climbing stairs, cycling the kids to school or walking to shops.

Mood diary for today:

	6am	8am	10am	12pm	2pm	4pm	6pm	8pm	10 pm	12 am	2am	4am
+5												
+4												
+3												
+2												
+1												
0												
-1												
-2												
-3												
-4												
-5												

Chart your mood with a cross or star either once or over the day.

Social contacts today:

Time	Who did you socialise with? Who are they to you?	How long for?	How do you feel?

Includes contacts at sports/gym, work, home and regular people you see during the day.

How did today go?

_____

_____

_____

What was the worst thing about today? _____

Did you talk with someone about this?   No   Yes

What was the **best thing** about today? _____

Did you talk with someone about this?   No   Yes

"Why fit in, when you were born to stand out." Dr Seuss

Today is _____ Date: _____

Food diary for today: (include any alcohol intake)

Time	Meal	Food	How do you feel?
	Breakfast		
	Morning tea		
	Lunch		
	Afternoon tea		
	Dinner		
	Supper		
	Extra snacks		

Sleep diary:

How many hours?	Quality?	Notes

Rested/tired/restless/interruptions/dreams/thirsty/toilet/worrying/crying?

Exercise diary for today:

Time	Exercise type	How long for?	How do you feel?

Include incidental exercise like climbing stairs, cycling the kids to school or walking to shops.

Mood diary for today:

	6am	8am	10am	12pm	2pm	4pm	6pm	8pm	10 pm	12 am	2am	4am
+5												
+4												
+3												
+2												
+1												
0												
-1												
-2												
-3												
-4												
-5												

Chart your mood with a cross or star either once or over the day.

Social contacts today:

Time	Who did you socialise with? Who are they to you?	How long for?	How do you feel?

Includes contacts at sports/gym, work, home and regular people you see during the day.

How did today go?

_____

_____

_____

What was the worst thing about today? _____

Did you talk with someone about this?   No   Yes

What was the **best thing** about today? _____

Did you talk with someone about this?   No   Yes

"Dream your dream first." Unknown

161

Today is _____ Date: _____

Food diary for today: (include any alcohol intake)

Time	Meal	Food	How do you feel?
	Breakfast		
	Morning tea		
	Lunch		
	Afternoon tea		
	Dinner		
	Supper		
	Extra snacks		

Sleep diary:

How many hours?	Quality?	Notes

Rested/tired/restless/interruptions/dreams/thirsty/toilet/worrying/crying?

Exercise diary for today:

Time	Exercise type	How long for?	How do you feel?

Include incidental exercise like climbing stairs, cycling the kids to school or walking to shops.

Mood diary for today:

	6am	8am	10am	12pm	2pm	4pm	6pm	8pm	10 pm	12 am	2am	4am
+5												
+4												
+3												
+2												
+1												
0												
-1												
-2												
-3												
-4												
-5												

Chart your mood with a cross or star either once or over the day.

Social contacts today:

Time	Who did you socialise with? Who are they to you?	How long for?	How do you feel?

Includes contacts at sports/gym, work, home and regular people you see during the day.

How did today go?

_____

_____

_____

What was the worst thing about today? _____

Did you talk with someone about this?   No   Yes

What was the **best thing** about today? _____

Did you talk with someone about this?   No   Yes

"When nothing goes right, try going left
and see what happens.' Unknown

Today is _____ Date: _____

Food diary for today: (include any alcohol intake)

Time	Meal	Food	How do you feel?
	Breakfast		
	Morning tea		
	Lunch		
	Afternoon tea		
	Dinner		
	Supper		
	Extra snacks		

Sleep diary:

How many hours?	Quality?	Notes

Rested/tired/restless/interruptions/dreams/thirsty/toilet/worrying/crying?

Exercise diary for today:

Time	Exercise type	How long for?	How do you feel?

Include incidental exercise like climbing stairs, cycling the kids to school or walking to shops.

Mood diary for today:

	6am	8am	10am	12pm	2pm	4pm	6pm	8pm	10 pm	12 am	2am	4am
+5												
+4												
+3												
+2												
+1												
0												
-1												
-2												
-3												
-4												
-5												

Chart your mood with a cross or star either once or over the day.

Social contacts today:

Time	Who did you socialise with? Who are they to you?	How long for?	How do you feel?

Includes contacts at sports/gym, work, home and regular people you see during the day.

How did today go?

_____

_____

_____

What was the worst thing about today? _____

Did you talk with someone about this?   No   Yes

What was the **best thing** about today? _____

Did you talk with someone about this?   No   Yes

_____

"The secret of getting ahead, is getting started." Agatha Christie

Today is _____ Date: _____

Food diary for today: (include any alcohol intake)

Time	Meal	Food	How do you feel?
	Breakfast		
	Morning tea		
	Lunch		
	Afternoon tea		
	Dinner		
	Supper		
	Extra snacks		

Sleep diary:

How many hours?	Quality?	Notes

Rested/tired/restless/interruptions/dreams/thirsty/toilet/worrying/crying?

Exercise diary for today:

Time	Exercise type	How long for?	How do you feel?

Include incidental exercise like climbing stairs, cycling the kids to school or walking to shops.

Mood diary for today:

	6am	8am	10am	12pm	2pm	4pm	6pm	8pm	10 pm	12 am	2am	4am
+5												
+4												
+3												
+2												
+1												
0												
-1												
-2												
-3												
-4												
-5												

Chart your mood with a cross or star either once or over the day.

Social contacts today:

Time	Who did you socialise with? Who are they to you?	How long for?	How do you feel?

Includes contacts at sports/gym, work, home and regular people you see during the day.

How did today go?

_____

_____

_____

What was the worst thing about today? _____

Did you talk with someone about this?   No   Yes

What was the **best thing** about today? _____

Did you talk with someone about this?   No   Yes

"Never let your loyalty make a fool of you." Unknown

Today is _____ Date: _____

Food diary for today: (include any alcohol intake)

Time	Meal	Food	How do you feel?
	Breakfast		
	Morning tea		
	Lunch		
	Afternoon tea		
	Dinner		
	Supper		
	Extra snacks		

Sleep diary:

How many hours?	Quality?	Notes

Rested/tired/restless/interruptions/dreams/thirsty/toilet/worrying/crying?

Exercise diary for today:

Time	Exercise type	How long for?	How do you feel?

Include incidental exercise like climbing stairs, cycling the kids to school or walking to shops.

Mood diary for today:

	6am	8am	10am	12pm	2pm	4pm	6pm	8pm	10 pm	12 am	2am	4am
+5												
+4												
+3												
+2												
+1												
0												
-1												
-2												
-3												
-4												
-5												

Chart your mood with a cross or star either once or over the day.

Social contacts today:

Time	Who did you socialise with? Who are they to you?	How long for?	How do you feel?

Includes contacts at sports/gym, work, home and regular people you see during the day.

How did today go?

_____

_____

_____

What was the worst thing about today? _____

Did you talk with someone about this?   No   Yes

What was the **best thing** about today? _____

Did you talk with someone about this?   No   Yes

"You can't change what's going on around you, until you have changed what is going on within you." Unknown

Today is _____ Date: _____

Food diary for today: (include any alcohol intake)

Time	Meal	Food	How do you feel?
	Breakfast		
	Morning tea		
	Lunch		
	Afternoon tea		
	Dinner		
	Supper		
	Extra snacks		

Sleep diary:

How many hours?	Quality?	Notes

Rested/tired/restless/interruptions/dreams/thirsty/toilet/worrying/crying?

Exercise diary for today:

Time	Exercise type	How long for?	How do you feel?

Include incidental exercise like climbing stairs, cycling the kids to school or walking to shops.

Mood diary for today:

	6am	8am	10am	12pm	2pm	4pm	6pm	8pm	10 pm	12 am	2am	4am
+5												
+4												
+3												
+2												
+1												
0												
-1												
-2												
-3												
-4												
-5												

Chart your mood with a cross or star either once or over the day.

Social contacts today:

Time	Who did you socialise with? Who are they to you?	How long for?	How do you feel?

Includes contacts at sports/gym, work, home and regular people you see during the day.

How did today go?

_____

_____

_____

What was the worst thing about today? _____

Did you talk with someone about this?   No   Yes

What was the **best thing** about today? _____

Did you talk with someone about this?   No   Yes

"Breathe in. Breathe out. Breathe." Chrystal V Benson

Today is _____ Date: _____

Food diary for today: (include any alcohol intake)

Time	Meal	Food	How do you feel?
	Breakfast		
	Morning tea		
	Lunch		
	Afternoon tea		
	Dinner		
	Supper		
	Extra snacks		

Sleep diary:

How many hours?	Quality?	Notes

Rested/tired/restless/interruptions/dreams/thirsty/toilet/worrying/crying?

Exercise diary for today:

Time	Exercise type	How long for?	How do you feel?

Include incidental exercise like climbing stairs, cycling the kids to school or walking to shops.

Mood diary for today:

	6am	8am	10am	12pm	2pm	4pm	6pm	8pm	10 pm	12 am	2am	4am
+5												
+4												
+3												
+2												
+1												
0												
-1												
-2												
-3												
-4												
-5												

Chart your mood with a cross or star either once or over the day.

Social contacts today:

Time	Who did you socialise with? Who are they to you?	How long for?	How do you feel?

Includes contacts at sports/gym, work, home and regular people you see during the day.

How did today go?

_____

_____

_____

What was the worst thing about today? _____

Did you talk with someone about this?   No   Yes

What was the **best thing** about today? _____

Did you talk with someone about this?   No   Yes

"If you don't stand for something, you will fall for anything." Peter Marshall

Today is _____ Date: _____

Food diary for today: (include any alcohol intake)

Time	Meal	Food	How do you feel?
	Breakfast		
	Morning tea		
	Lunch		
	Afternoon tea		
	Dinner		
	Supper		
	Extra snacks		

Sleep diary:

How many hours?	Quality?	Notes

Rested/tired/restless/interruptions/dreams/thirsty/toilet/worrying/crying?

Exercise diary for today:

Time	Exercise type	How long for?	How do you feel?

Include incidental exercise like climbing stairs, cycling the kids to school or walking to shops.

Mood diary for today:

	6am	8am	10am	12pm	2pm	4pm	6pm	8pm	10 pm	12 am	2am	4am
+5												
+4												
+3												
+2												
+1												
0												
-1												
-2												
-3												
-4												
-5												

Chart your mood with a cross or star either once or over the day.

Social contacts today:

Time	Who did you socialise with? Who are they to you?	How long for?	How do you feel?

Includes contacts at sports/gym, work, home and regular people you see during the day.

How did today go?

_____

_____

_____

What was the worst thing about today? _____

Did you talk with someone about this?   No   Yes

What was the **best thing** about today? _____

Did you talk with someone about this?   No   Yes

_____

"Your potential grows with each lesson learnt." Unknown

Today is _____ Date: _____

Food diary for today: (include any alcohol intake)

Time	Meal	Food	How do you feel?
	Breakfast		
	Morning tea		
	Lunch		
	Afternoon tea		
	Dinner		
	Supper		
	Extra snacks		

Sleep diary:

How many hours?	Quality?	Notes

Rested/tired/restless/interruptions/dreams/thirsty/toilet/worrying/crying?

Exercise diary for today:

Time	Exercise type	How long for?	How do you feel?

Include incidental exercise like climbing stairs, cycling the kids to school or walking to shops.

Mood diary for today:

	6am	8am	10am	12pm	2pm	4pm	6pm	8pm	10 pm	12 am	2am	4am
+5												
+4												
+3												
+2												
+1												
0												
-1												
-2												
-3												
-4												
-5												

Chart your mood with a cross or star either once or over the day.

Social contacts today:

Time	Who did you socialise with? Who are they to you?	How long for?	How do you feel?

Includes contacts at sports/gym, work, home and regular people you see during the day.

How did today go?

_____

_____

_____

What was the worst thing about today? _____

Did you talk with someone about this?   No   Yes

What was the **best thing** about today? _____

Did you talk with someone about this?   No   Yes

_____

"The worst thing you can do to someone with an invisible illness, is make them feel like they need to prove how sick they are." Unknown

Today is _____ Date: _____

Food diary for today: (include any alcohol intake)

Time	Meal	Food	How do you feel?
	Breakfast		
	Morning tea		
	Lunch		
	Afternoon tea		
	Dinner		
	Supper		
	Extra snacks		

Sleep diary:

How many hours?	Quality?	Notes

Rested/tired/restless/interruptions/dreams/thirsty/toilet/worrying/crying?

Exercise diary for today:

Time	Exercise type	How long for?	How do you feel?

Include incidental exercise like climbing stairs, cycling the kids to school or walking to shops.

Mood diary for today:

	6am	8am	10am	12pm	2pm	4pm	6pm	8pm	10 pm	12 am	2am	4am
+5												
+4												
+3												
+2												
+1												
0												
-1												
-2												
-3												
-4												
-5												

Chart your mood with a cross or star either once or over the day.

Social contacts today:

Time	Who did you socialise with? Who are they to you?	How long for?	How do you feel?

Includes contacts at sports/gym, work, home and regular people you see during the day.

How did today go?

_____

_____

_____

What was the worst thing about today? _____

Did you talk with someone about this?   No   Yes

What was the **best thing** about today? _____

Did you talk with someone about this?   No   Yes

"Never give up on someone with mental illness. When the "I" is replaced with "WE", illness becomes wellness." Shannon L Alder

Today is _____ Date: _____

Food diary for today: (include any alcohol intake)

Time	Meal	Food	How do you feel?
	Breakfast		
	Morning tea		
	Lunch		
	Afternoon tea		
	Dinner		
	Supper		
	Extra snacks		

Sleep diary:

How many hours?	Quality?	Notes

Rested/tired/restless/interruptions/dreams/thirsty/toilet/worrying/crying?

Exercise diary for today:

Time	Exercise type	How long for?	How do you feel?

Include incidental exercise like climbing stairs, cycling the kids to school or walking to shops.

Mood diary for today:

	6am	8am	10am	12pm	2pm	4pm	6pm	8pm	10 pm	12 am	2am	4am
+5												
+4												
+3												
+2												
+1												
0												
-1												
-2												
-3												
-4												
-5												

Chart your mood with a cross or star either once or over the day.

Social contacts today:

Time	Who did you socialise with? Who are they to you?	How long for?	How do you feel?

Includes contacts at sports/gym, work, home and regular people you see during the day.

How did today go?

_____

_____

_____

What was the worst thing about today? _____

Did you talk with someone about this?   No   Yes

What was the **best thing** about today? _____

Did you talk with someone about this?   No   Yes

"Come what come may, time and the hour runs through the roughest day." Macbeth – William Shakespeare

Today is _____ Date: _____

Food diary for today: (include any alcohol intake)

Time	Meal	Food	How do you feel?
	Breakfast		
	Morning tea		
	Lunch		
	Afternoon tea		
	Dinner		
	Supper		
	Extra snacks		

Sleep diary:

How many hours?	Quality?	Notes

Rested/tired/restless/interruptions/dreams/thirsty/toilet/worrying/crying?

Exercise diary for today:

Time	Exercise type	How long for?	How do you feel?

Include incidental exercise like climbing stairs, cycling the kids to school or walking to shops.

Mood diary for today:

	6am	8am	10am	12pm	2pm	4pm	6pm	8pm	10 pm	12 am	2am	4am
+5												
+4												
+3												
+2												
+1												
0												
-1												
-2												
-3												
-4												
-5												

Chart your mood with a cross or star either once or over the day.

Social contacts today:

Time	Who did you socialise with? Who are they to you?	How long for?	How do you feel?

Includes contacts at sports/gym, work, home and regular people you see during the day.

How did today go?

_____

_____

_____

What was the worst thing about today? _____

Did you talk with someone about this?   No   Yes

What was the **best thing** about today? _____

Did you talk with someone about this?   No   Yes

"The most wasted of all days is one without laughter."
Nicolas Chamfort

Today is _____ Date: _____

Food diary for today: (include any alcohol intake)

Time	Meal	Food	How do you feel?
	Breakfast		
	Morning tea		
	Lunch		
	Afternoon tea		
	Dinner		
	Supper		
	Extra snacks		

Sleep diary:

How many hours?	Quality?	Notes

Rested/tired/restless/interruptions/dreams/thirsty/toilet/worrying/crying?

Exercise diary for today:

Time	Exercise type	How long for?	How do you feel?

Include incidental exercise like climbing stairs, cycling the kids to school or walking to shops.

Mood diary for today:

	6am	8am	10am	12pm	2pm	4pm	6pm	8pm	10 pm	12 am	2am	4am
+5												
+4												
+3												
+2												
+1												
0												
-1												
-2												
-3												
-4												
-5												

Chart your mood with a cross or star either once or over the day.

Social contacts today:

Time	Who did you socialise with? Who are they to you?	How long for?	How do you feel?

Includes contacts at sports/gym, work, home and regular people you see during the day.

How did today go?

_____

_____

_____

What was the worst thing about today? _____

Did you talk with someone about this?   No   Yes

What was the **best thing** about today? _____

Did you talk with someone about this?   No   Yes

"Prepare and prevent, don't repair and repent." Unknown

Today is _____ Date: _____

Food diary for today: (include any alcohol intake)

Time	Meal	Food	How do you feel?
	Breakfast		
	Morning tea		
	Lunch		
	Afternoon tea		
	Dinner		
	Supper		
	Extra snacks		

Sleep diary:

How many hours?	Quality?	Notes

Rested/tired/restless/interruptions/dreams/thirsty/toilet/worrying/crying?

Exercise diary for today:

Time	Exercise type	How long for?	How do you feel?

Include incidental exercise like climbing stairs, cycling the kids to school or walking to shops.

Mood diary for today:

	6am	8am	10am	12pm	2pm	4pm	6pm	8pm	10 pm	12 am	2am	4am
+5												
+4												
+3												
+2												
+1												
0												
-1												
-2												
-3												
-4												
-5												

Chart your mood with a cross or star either once or over the day.

Social contacts today:

Time	Who did you socialise with? Who are they to you?	How long for?	How do you feel?

Includes contacts at sports/gym, work, home and regular people you see during the day.

How did today go?

_____

_____

_____

What was the worst thing about today? _____

Did you talk with someone about this?   No   Yes

What was the **best thing** about today? _____

Did you talk with someone about this?   No   Yes

_____

"Ships in harbours are safe. But that is not what ships are built for." Unknown

Extra Diary Page

Today is _____ Date: _____

Food diary for today: (include any alcohol intake)

Time	Meal	Food	How do you feel?
	Breakfast		
	Morning tea		
	Lunch		
	Afternoon tea		
	Dinner		
	Supper		
	Extra snacks		

Sleep diary:

How many hours?	Quality?	Notes

Rested/tired/restless/interruptions/dreams/thirsty/toilet/worrying/crying?

Exercise diary for today:

Time	Exercise type	How long for?	How do you feel?

Include incidental exercise like climbing stairs, cycling the kids to school or walking to shops.

Mood diary for today:

	6am	8am	10am	12pm	2pm	4pm	6pm	8pm	10 pm	12 am	2am	4am
+5												
+4												
+3												
+2												
+1												
0												
-1												
-2												
-3												
-4												
-5												

Chart your mood with a cross or star either once or over the day.

Social contacts today:

Time	Who did you socialise with? Who are they to you?	How long for?	How do you feel?

Includes contacts at sports/gym, work, home and regular people you see during the day.

How did today go?

_____

_____

_____

What was the worst thing about today? _____

Did you talk with someone about this?   No   Yes

What was the **best thing** about today? _____

Did you talk with someone about this?   No   Yes

"The beautiful thing about learning, is no one can take it away from you." BB King

Keeping Well Plan

Keeping Well Plan for _____ (your name) DOB _____

Early warning Symptoms and Signs

Symptoms are what you notice, signs are what others notice.

What do you notice when you are becoming unwell?	What do others notice when you are becoming unwell?	What do you want to happen now?

Who do you want to contact now?

Name of Person	Their role in your health	Phone number

Who has a copy of this plan?

Name of Person	Their role in your health	Phone number

Your Keeping Well Plan (on A5 file card)

Please create a card that you carry on you, try a A5 file card with lines on it to help keep your information close at hand. If you have a Case/Care Manager, ask them for the A5 file card.

Use both sides of the A5 file card as follows:

Front side of card:

Name:	Date of Plan:
I experience episodes of being unwell such as:	What I plan to do when this happens:

On the reverse side of the A5 file card write the following:

What I would like you to do when I am unwell is:	Contacts:
	My doctor is _____ Phone number_____
	My Case/Care Manager is _____ Phone number _____
If I am worried about my symptoms, I will call: Immediately _____ Phone number_____	If you are worried about the signs, please call: Name_____ Phone number _____ They are my _____

Talk to your family, friends, care/case manager and your Doctor about your keeping well plan and then give them all a copy, so you can have your voice heard. Remember though, if you are really unwell, you may need a more intensive intervention, so try to catch yourself before this occurs.

Your Relapse Prevention Plan

Relapse Prevention Plan

(it's like Your Keeping Well Plan but gives you some
more reminders of what to look out for).

Your name_____ Date_____

1. I have a mental health diagnosis called

2. When I am unwell, I experiences these symptoms:

3. I find these stressful situations to affect my mental health and I can become unwell

4. I will try these things to help when I am in a stressful situation

5. My current stressful situations seem to be

Relapse Prevention Plan

6. When I know that a stressful situation may happen I will try to reduce the stress levels by

7. I know I have many positive qualities, values and beliefs. They are

8. I have professional support, such as

Name	Their relationship to me	Phone number

9. I have supportive family and friends

Name	Their relationship to me	Phone number

10. Every day, I can care for myself by doing one of these activities and if I have time more than one

Printed in the United States
By Bookmasters